# God's Got Your Back

## Wisdom to reduce back-related pain caused by degenerative disc disease

Tammi E. Smorynski
1/23/2015

First Edition

Eleanor Publishing

San Jose, California

God's Got Your Back
By Tammi E. Smorynski
First Edition 2014

Published by Eleanor Publishing
5669 Snell #234
San Jose, CA 95123
EleanorPublishing@gmail.com

Copyright © 2014 by Tammi E. Smorynski

Edition ISBNs:
ISBN-9-780692-311837

Printed in the United States of America

Cover photographs by Ronald V. Smorynski
Photographs by Michael L. Craig

# Contents

In Memory of My Wisconsin Grandmother ................................ 3

Acknowledgements ........................................................ 5

Warning-Disclaimer ........................................................ 7

Chapter 1: Why a Christian Back Book? ........................... 9

Chapter 2: On Wisdom ................................................. 17

*Get Wisdom* ............................................................ 18

*Seek Jehovah-Rophe for Wisdom* ........................... 21

*Trust God to Provide Wisdom* ................................ 23

Chapter 3: The ABCs ................................................... 33

Chapter 4: The Process ................................................ 51

*Diagnosis* ............................................................... 53

*Healing/Rehabilitation* ........................................... 54

*Maintenance* .......................................................... 55

*Weather* ................................................................. 55

Chapter 5: Medications, Supplements and Surgery ....... 59

*Medication* ............................................................. 59

*Supplements* .......................................................... 62

*Surgery* .................................................................. 65

Chapter 6: Posture .......................................................... 69

Standing .................................................................. 71

Sitting..................................................................... 74

Sleeping ................................................................. 77

Other Posture-Related Items ..................................... 78

Chapter 7: The Temperature Packs ............................... 83

Heat ....................................................................... 84

Ice.......................................................................... 87

Chapter 8: Rehabilitation ............................................. 93

Adjustments............................................................ 94

Traction .................................................................. 94

Other Devices.......................................................... 97

Massages................................................................ 97

Other Techniques .................................................... 100

Chapter 9: Exercise..................................................... 105

Stretching................................................................ 108

Strengthening .......................................................... 115

Cardio .................................................................... 120

Chapter 10: Issues Not Addressed ................................ 123

Chapter 11: One Final Step .......................................... 127

Chapter 12: Concluding Remarks .................................. 129

Apendix A: Sample Worksheet...................................... 132

About the Author ........................................................ 133

Figure 1 - Wisconsin Grandmother

# In Memory of My Wisconsin Grandmother

Psalms 139:13-14
*For you created my inmost being; you knit me together in my mother's womb. I praise you because I am fearfully and wonderfully made; your works are wonderful, I know that full well.*

When I was young, I remember seeing my Grandmother grab the kitchen counter while standing in pain as another sciatic surge ran down her leg. She never complained to us about her back. I would just hear about her back pain from time to time. My Grandmother passed away six years before my back issues started. I wanted so much to talk to her about her back problems and how she dealt with it. When I started getting the surge down my leg, I would think of her and wonder would I too suffer my whole life—or were there new ways to deal with back issues?

My name is Tammi. Many people misspell my name as Tammy or Tammie. What makes this more confusing is that my middle initial is E. My dad does not recall why he and my mother chose my middle name. My mom chose it to feel part of his family. When I was young, I did not like telling people what the E stood for, as I felt it was so old-fashioned. I wanted E to stand for Elizabeth, but it didn't. Being born in Korea, I found it odd that my parents gave me that middle name vs. a Korean middle name.

Ever since I can remember, I have signed my name with the E in a pronounced way so people would not include it in my first name. Now when people ask me what it stands for, I proudly say it stands for Eleanor, after my Wisconsin Grandmother. My parents unwittingly named me after the person whose bone structure and back problems I inherited. I think of her fondly whenever I look at my hands and marvel at the wonders of God.

# Acknowledgements

Thank you God, for providing me with an amazing body that can heal itself and for helping me find the wisdom I have needed to deal with my back issues. I would be a complete mess if it weren't for your unfailing love and faithfulness in guiding me all these years.

Thank you as well to all the medical professionals who have helped me deal with my back issues since 2007— and to those who were not of much help, because you inspired me to find those who did help.

Thank you to Charles Von Hammerstein for spending time to educate me on self-publishing and referring me to Dan Poynter's book, "Self-Publishing", which provided many insights about the process. Thank you to Neil Mammen for his additional insights on self-publishing.

Thank you to my mom for pestering me to read the Bible, for walking with me as I have matured in my faith, and for praying for me and helping me as I dealt with my back problems. Thanks to my Uncle Tony for supplying me with a picture of my Grandmother to include in the book, my brother Mikey, who took the pictures for the book, to my brother Ronnie for reviewing my book and helping me with the cover and to my sister Sumi for feedback and encouragement.

Thank you to Pastor Ken Foreman, who inspired me to fulfill a life-long dream of writing a book. I wouldn't have started this project had I not been attending Cathedral of Faith, in San Jose, California, just as

Pastor Ken began his "Imagine Living Your Dream" sermon series.

I'm also grateful to Pastor Stephen Furtick (who I've never met) for his two books, "*Sun Stand Still*", and "*Greater*", which pricked my soul to press in to the greater life God has for me.

Thanks to all my friends who prayed for me, gave me advice and laughed with me as I stumbled through the process of dealing with my back issues and writing this book. Thanks especially to Karen Schmidt for praying for me and pointing me back to God and the Bible for healing. Karen's words and email are what lead me to the premise of this book.

Thanks to Larry Haise for being the first person to read my book! I appreciate your meticulous attention to editing my book to make it easier to read. I was humbled by your positive comments and encouragement to get it published.

Thanks to J. Carpenter, J. Olbeda and M. Janzen who read my book, provided suggestions and confirmed via their comments that my main points/thoughts were being relayed to them as intended.

# Warning-Disclaimer

This book is meant to share my experience in managing my specific back issues. It is in no way meant to prescribe a specific program for all back issues. Nor is this book meant to provide a diagnosis and treatment plan for any specific person. For a diagnosis and specific treatment plan, you should consult medical professionals and, of course, lay your request before God for his divine help.

This book is written by someone who does not have a medical degree or certification. It is based solely on her personal back experience. The book does not contain all the medical information about back issues. You are encouraged to read all available material to become educated on this topic and to talk to medical professionals for their perspective, especially when it comes to your specific back problem.

This text should be used only as a general guide and may contain typographical and content mistakes.

"The purpose of this manual is to educate and entertain. The author and Eleanor Publishing shall have neither liability nor responsibility to any person or entity with respect to any loss or damage caused, or alleged to have been caused, directly or indirectly, by the information contained in this book. If you do not wish to be bound by the above, you may return the book to the publisher for a full refund."[1]

---

[1] Except for the phrase "and Eleanor Publishing", this material is quoted from "Self-Publishing Manual" by Dan Poynter.

# Chapter 1

# Why a Christian Back Book?

### Mark 5:25-34

*And a woman was there who had been subject to bleeding for twelve years. She had suffered a great deal under the care of many doctors and had spent all she had, yet instead of getting better she grew worse. When she heard about Jesus, she came up behind him in the crowd and touched his cloak, because she thought, "If I just touch his clothes, I will be healed." Immediately her bleeding stopped and she felt in her body that she was freed from her suffering. At once Jesus realized that power had gone out from him. He turned around in the crowd and asked, "Who touched my clothes?"*

*"You see the people crowding against you," his disciples answered, "and yet you can ask, 'Who touched me?'"*
*But Jesus kept looking around to see who had done it. Then the woman, knowing what had happened to her, came and fell at his feet and, trembling with fear, told him the whole truth. He said to her, "Daughter, your faith has healed you. Go in peace and be freed from your suffering."*

In the Jewish culture a woman was considered unclean during her monthly cycle. She was not allowed to come into the temple or be around people, especially during special holiday celebrations. This woman had

9

been dealing with a bleeding issue for 12 years, which meant she could not enter the temple for 12 years. I can't imagine missing two straight weeks of church, let alone 12 years. She was estranged from those around her, either by their knowledge of her situation or her fear of being found out. Back then, people with "skin and bleeding diseases" were separated from their community. So she likely lived in complete fear and desperately sought a solution. The Bible says she spent all she had trying to deal with this issue, with no relief. When she found out that Jesus was in the neighborhood, something inside of her let her know that if she could but touch his garment, she would be healed. In panic, fear, distress, anxiety and desperation, she went to find him, and, seeing him in a crowd, pressed in to touch him.

I have heard this short story in many sermons about faith, but it has never meant as much to me as it did when I began to have back issues and that I might be just like this woman. Would I too spend all I had to deal with my issue? How could I touch Jesus' garment today? How could I receive a healing miracle like this woman's? *Will God be merciful to me?*

Today, thankfully, we have a broader perspective on health issues and for the most part, don't isolate people. We don't keep people out of church. In fact, many pastors and laypeople visit those who can't make it to church. Many of us have had medical issues that drag on for years, and we have wondered if we would ever get better. And many of us have tried this or that remedy, spending time searching for answers, spending money seeing medical professionals, and spending more time trying various approaches, only to hit points of despair as the health issue remained and the situation seemed hopeless. Then, after a few days, we revive our hope and begin the search again and, if we can afford it, see yet another specialist or read another book or try another treatment in hope of finding that elusive cure. Maybe we even visit a Christian healing place. At last, when we can't stand it any longer and feel completely helpless, we turn to God. We cry out for help and ask people to pray for us. *God has been merciful to me.*

I am not a medical doctor nor have I had any formal medical training. I am just a person living my life and trying to relay information I have gathered and share lessons I have learned on my journey. If you find this book useful in any way, praise God. If you disagree, that is good too, and hopefully you will get more informed on that area and make your own decisions and maybe even write your own book. *God has been merciful to me.*

I'm sure many of us today wish we could touch Jesus' garment and be healed. Like the woman in Mark's Gospel, we have spent many months and years visiting this or that doctor and trying this or that treatment to no avail. *God has been merciful to me.*

When my back first went out, I was in complete shock. Would I suffer like my grandma or find healing? As I trudged through my memory banks trying to remember people I knew who had back problems, and how they dealt with them and are dealing with them, I was left feeling a bit at a loss. Pain, pain pills and taking time off from work were all the solutions tried that I could remember. When I contacted people with back issues, they said I'd be taking pain pills for the rest of my life and might need to try surgery with no guarantee of being out of pain. I remember sitting in a spine specialist's office and seeing all the people with pain written on their faces, and it was not just temporary pain. I could see that they had been in pain for some time. *God has been merciful to me.*

As you'll read later, my problem started small and quickly worsened. My mother later told me she thought I would become incapacitated by the pain or by pain medications. I was certain there was a better way—there just had to be. My mother also told me she was amazed that during the worst part I never missed church or participating in the various ministries in which I was involved. I took time off from work to visit medical professionals but kept working through it all. *God has been merciful to me.*

As I began the journey, I started with medical doctors. I never even imagined going to a chiropractor, as I thought they were quacks. However, when you are in pain and you get desperate, you will try a lot of crazy things. Fortunately, going to a chiropractor is not crazy. *God has been merciful to me.*

My chiropractor directed me to other care professionals. I was blessed in being able to talk to many people and get different opinions. I know that many people cannot afford the money or effort to get all the information I have gathered. I hope this information will help you maximize every visit to medical health practitioners. *God has been merciful to me.*

This book is about my journey to deal with my specific back issues. My back issues may be the polar opposite of your experience. I am not writing to say my way is the only way and the right way. I am writing to give you information and let you determine what is right for you in your situation, from both a financial and time perspective. Even if you only adapt one suggestion of mine into your daily routine, you will be doing better than just running to doctors, taking lots of medications and avoiding activity, and then a year later doing the same thing. I hope that by reading this book you will be better equipped to ask questions and determine for yourself the right path to take when you consult medical professionals. Don't get me wrong. If you receive a prescription for medication, you should follow the doctor's advice—subject to a point I make in later section, "Medication, Supplements and Surgery". You should NOT assume all your medical professionals are divinely knowledgeable—that they are somehow perfect in understanding—because they are not. They are human after all. I challenged the spine specialist on his interpretation of my back problem, and my MRI proved me right and him wrong. (More on this is coming.) *God has been merciful to me.*

When you have your first disc issue, you want to believe it is a one-time experience. Within the first year of dealing with my lower back issue, I started having pain in my neck area. The chiropractor warned me that this would be a lifelong back management process. At first I did not want to accept this message. However, when my neck, shoulder, arm and hand started having sensations of pain and tightness, I knew he was right. I had a choice—do nothing and wait for each flare-up or be proactive to minimize the number and intensity of each flare-up episode. I decided to be proactive. After seven years, I've had one major lower back and one major neck flare-up, each lasting around two months—far shorter than the first full year I spent suffering from my back problems. I have had a number of minor flare-ups, each lasting a day or two. *God has been merciful to me.*

I will never get to share what I have learned with my grandma, but I can share it with you and with others to encourage you that you do not have to live in constant pain, taking tons of pills, going through a surgery, and having to take time off from work, or worse, going onto medical disability because of all the pain and medications. God's hand is all over my journey, so to tell what I know without including God would be like telling the story about the woman above without explaining why all of a sudden the bleeding stopped. The whole point is that we will all likely suffer various health issues in our lifetimes, but if we focus on Jesus, He can show us the best pathway. *God has been merciful to me.*

For those experiencing your first back pain and those who have suffered many years, I fervently hope and pray that this book will give you ideas for addressing your back problems without going broke. The first step in this process is to turn to Jesus. I thank God every day that this is part of what I did. You'll learn shortly that it was God's divine intent that I had no other choice but to turn to him. And though I saw several medical professionals and tried various remedies, I know my time in pain and on medications has been vastly less than for others. I have learned so much that I feel compelled to share it so others might find the answers they need faster. *May God be merciful to YOU!*

## Next Steps:

1. Take a deep breath.
2. Do not try to rush through this book. Take time to consider the material in each chapter including the Next Steps.

## Prayer:

Father, I pray for people who read this book—that they will learn more about You while they learn how to better manage their back issues. I pray that You will be merciful to them as they draw close to You, as You have been merciful to me. I thank You knowing You will use this book to help Your people. Thank You! In Jesus' name, Amen.

# Chapter 2

# **On Wisdom**

Proverbs 3:13

*Blessed are those who find wisdom, those who gain understanding.*

Proverbs 4:7

*The beginning of wisdom is this: Get wisdom. Though it cost all you have, get understanding.*

Proverbs 16:16

*How much better to get wisdom than gold, to get insight rather than silver!*

Proverbs 19:8

*The one who gets wisdom loves life; the one cherishes understanding will soon prosper.*

Proverbs 23:12

*Apply your heart to instruction and your ears to words of knowledge.*

Knowledge: "The state or fact of knowing."[2]

Wisdom: "The ability to discern or judge what is true, right or lasting."[3]

Many people know things, e.g. have knowledge, but they do not have the wisdom to use that knowledge correctly. The book of Proverbs tells us over and over to seek wisdom and that God has made it readily available for those that would seek it and cherish it. And yet, we often think we are wise in our own eyes and try to do things based on our finite understanding. We need to humble ourselves, being open to learn new things and seek to understand. Do not rely on others to tell you how to manage your back. Rely on God to lead you through this process.

### Get Wisdom

When my back went out in 2007, it happened over a series of events. I first strained it after playing a gazillion games of volleyball. I proceeded to use the heater in my car seat, thinking that if I warmed my back, it would feel better. Stupid!!! The heat felt great, but once I got out of my car, my back hurt worse. I did not realize it, but the heat was inflaming my back more than it was already inflamed. I called the doctor's office and the nurse told me to not use any heat for 24-48 hours. She got me on the right track with ice and ibuprofen. About five weeks later, I went on a mission

---

[2] http://www.thefreedictionary.com/wisdom
[3] http://www.thefreedictionary.com/wisdom

trip to Ethiopia. That meant sitting on a plane for more than 20 hours, and this is when the real pain began. You don't want your back to go out during a mission trip in a place where there is no ice, where you are having food issues so can't take much medication and where there is no real medical help. I spent 15 days in Ethiopia in pain. I had no choice but to pray to God and ask for his help. I prayed desperately for immediate healing but didn't get that. So I scrambled for what to pray for since I was desperate. I decided to pray for wisdom for what to do. And because I'm a bit of a wimp on the pain scale, I prayed for endurance, to be able to bear up under the pain until I got home and could get medical help. I asked everyone on our mission trip to pray for me.

And do you know what? God answered my prayers. People started sharing with me what helped them with pain or helped someone they knew who struggled with pain. I began trying out stretches, used my clothes to make my bed flatter and took long walks every day, though at the time walking seemed counterintuitive. Following the various recommendations, I was able to get my pain way down.

About five weeks after returning home, I took another plane trip, and my pain went south again— literally south, as it descended down my spine to my tailbone. This time I had doctors, medication, food and ice, but the process was overwhelming and the pain continued to get worse even with help. Again out of complete desperation I prayed for healing and if not healing wisdom and if not wisdom then endurance. I've since prayed this prayer many times about my back and other health issues. And you know what? God has answered my prayers.

Back issues can plague you for decades, so why try to do this on your own when God tells us to seek Him for wisdom?

James 1:5 *If any of you lacks **wisdom**, you should ask God, who **gives** generously to all without finding fault, and it will be given to you.*

Proverbs 2:6 *For the Lord **gives wisdom**; from his mouth come knowledge and understanding.*

Proverbs 3:5-8 *Trust in the Lord with all your heart and lean not on your own understanding; in all your ways submit to him, and he will make your paths straight. **Do not be wise in your own eyes**; fear the Lord and shun evil. This will bring **health** to your body and nourishment to your bones.*

Proverbs 4:5 ***Get wisdom**, get understanding; do not forget my words or turn away from them.*

*(I have put key words in **boldface** for emphasis.)*

I kept finding out about people with neck and back issues. I would try to share what I had learned, but there is only so much you can cover in a quick chat or even an hour. After the fifth conversation like this, I felt annoyed, as I knew I had more information to share with them that would help them. But neither they nor I had the time to talk further then. I kept thinking that I should write it down and just email the information to people, but I knew even a two-page document wasn't sufficient. This book grew out of the desire to share what I had learned to help other people struggling with pain caused by back problems. This book is the wisdom God has imparted to me to manage my back. I hope it will help you manage yours too.

## Seek Jehovah-Rophe for Wisdom

It is vital that you understand which God I'm talking about because it makes all the difference in what to expect. I'm talking about the God of the Bible, the God of Abraham, Isaac and Jacob—the God who is three in one, God the Father, God the Son and God the Holy Spirit and the God who identifies himself in the Bible as the great "I AM." He is known by many names. When it comes to health issues, Christians and Jews steeped in the Scriptures will tell you about God's healing name: Jehovah-Rophe, which means "God heals."

*"The word "rophe" appears some sixty or seventy times in the Old Testament, always meaning "to restore," "to heal," "to cure," as a physician, not only in the physical sense but in the moral and spiritual sense also."*[4]

I believe that the Bible is the inspired word of God and that what it says is true. I believe God provided miraculous healings in ancient times and still heals today. I believe in the promises of the Bible, so I trust that when I call on—pray to—Him, He hears me and will work on my behalf as a good father on earth does to help me. If you are not a Christian, I still think you will get some help by reading this book, but it may not all make sense to you.

---

[4] http://www.justthetruth.net/The%20Names%20Of%20God.htm, 6) Jehovah-Rophe

Whenever I have a medical issue, and trust me, I've had my fair share, I first get overwhelmed and then I remind myself of these simple truths:

1) This challenge for me did not catch God by surprise. He is already moving on my behalf in the situation.

2) God is still Jehovah-Rophe and can heal me. He may choose not to for many reasons. He is not a genie in a bottle. He is God, and He may want to correct some poor or uninformed choices I'm making that lead to the problem.

I once kept getting a weird rash on my neck. Had God healed it instantaneously, it would have just come back because I was unknowingly causing it. You might ask, "Couldn't God have cured the rash in such a way that your behavior didn't matter?" Yes, but then I would have had skin like an alligator, and I like my skin to be soft. It doesn't make sense that God would give me a miracle healing for something I would cause again. God did me a favor by not giving me the miracle I begged for, and instead He gave me wisdom to deal with it. You'll learn more about this situation later.

In re-reviewing the definition of Jehovah-Rophe, I came to an interesting realization. It relates to God as exhibiting behavior such as we expect from a physician or other medical professional. God is far more than this, as He can provide instantaneous miraculous healings. However, there are similarities between what physicians do and what God does. They help us find healing for our bodies. They use their education and experience to help us. We do not receive immediate healing by being in their presence or even by starting treatment programs they prescribe. In many respects they must impart wisdom to us to help us resolve our situation. Medical wisdom may involve changing behavior, taking medication, having surgery, exercising or changing diet. When we seek God for a healing, most of us are asking for a miracle only—that is, an instant healing. God is still in the miracle business, but He also imparts wisdom directly to us and indirectly through many paths like medical professionals. Are we willing to seek God for wisdom?

## *Trust God to Provide Wisdom*

When you look at how God healed various people in the Bible, you will notice that very few healings occurred in exactly the same way others did. In some, the person with the issue was required to participate in the process—to have faith and stand up if he was crippled, for example. In other situations people didn't even know what was going on. The boy the prophet Elijah brought back to life is an example. This tells me that God heals in different ways. So He is also likely to provide wisdom in different ways as well. He gave me the insight I needed to manage my specific back issues, and pointers from Him came in various ways. I believe you will need to consider doing things similar to what I did but not exactly the same. You must seek God's wisdom for your specific back issues. Be open to what He has to tell you about what to do.

First, you will need to pray about your situation. Second, you will need to believe God will help you in ways that are appropriate and an effective for you.

## *Pray*

This is obvious, I know, but how many times does something happen, we deal with it on our own and it doesn't go the way we wanted? We're crushed. We whine to family and friends. Then, when we have reached the end of ourselves, we scream out a quick HELP! to God. God hears this plea, but we could save ourselves a lot of heartache and pain if we would make prayer a regular part of our day and life.

When my back first went out, I wasn't praying on a regular basis. I would pray only when things got really, really bad. I will always wonder how much of the pain I went through would have been curtailed if I had been asking God for wisdom sooner.

So how should you pray? First, be honest with God about yourself. Are you living in accord with His Word and will for your life? Or are you living in direct opposition to what you know you should be doing? If you are a Christian choosing to do things you know you should not be doing like—lying, cheating, committing adultery and the like—I believe your prayers may be bouncing off the ceiling. Be attentive to areas that God wants you to turn from or address in your life as part of this process. The truth is no one can live a perfectly sinless life. That is why God has provided help even on this through Jesus's sacrifice for us. Have you accepted Jesus' free gift? If not and you want to know more about this, see Chapter 11.

Once you acknowledge your sin and humble yourself before Almighty God, you can pray boldly to Him for help, knowing He hears you and wants the best for you.

I was delayed and delayed in getting to this chapter to edit. When I finally found the time, I found it was a mess. I kept adding stuff as God was revealing it to me, and it became disorganized. Two things happened, and it was if God delayed me so that when I was editing this chapter I would have new insights to pour in to it.

First, I was watching a Joyce Meyer TV show in which she reminded viewers about the Holy Spirit's help. How often have we had that feeling in our gut that we should do something and we didn't do it—and not doing it caused problems? And then we go to the doctor and he or she will tell us to do what we know we should have been doing all along. When we pray, we should be asking God to help us better discern what the Holy Spirit is trying to communicate to us. This is how God imparts wisdom to us, through the Holy Spirit, also known as the Comforter. If we are not aware of or paying attention to the Holy Spirit, we may very well miss the answers to our prayers.

When I was dealing with the previously mentioned rash on my neck, I did ask for wisdom, but then I tried to solve the problem myself. I looked at what shampoos I was using, what food I was eating and what laundry detergent I was using. I tried many combinations to see if I could figure what was causing the rash. I went to the doctor often and researched online. Finally, after a couple of years, I gave up my search for a cause and cure. I said, "Okay, God, I guess you are not going to take this away or show me how to take it away. I give up. I'll do my best to manage this and believe that at the right time you'll make it clear to me what I should do." I mentally pushed the problem over to God and found a lot of peace. I went about my day and then, when I was resting on my bed, my neck flared up again. I relooked at the rash, and this time it seemed as if it might have been caused by friction. Then it came to me. I was causing my rash. (More on this later.) When I finally quieted my mind, the Holy Spirit could speak to me and show me what the problem was. Do you have a minor health issue that you have tried everything to resolve and gotten nowhere? Give it over to God. Let it go. Quiet your mind. Let the Holy Spirit bring you the answer in God's timing.

Second, I got a nasty sore throat. After two days of gargling salt water, sucking on zinc lozenges, taking vitamin C and Tylenol, eating chicken noodle soup, drinking tons of water and sleeping as much as possible, my throat seemed to be getting worse, not better. So I went to the doctor. Before I went in, I prayed for wisdom and discernment to help with this situation. This was an unusual sore throat, as there was no congestion or cough or other symptoms apart from pain and a fever. The strep test came back negative. The doctor was just going to have me "tough it out." Right toward the end of the appointment I asked if I should continue with the Tylenol for the fever or switch to something else. She said something like "Oh, I didn't realize you had a fever too. Let's get you started on antibiotics." It was four days after I started the antibiotics before I was out of pain—and day six since my throat had started hurting. It was clearly some sort of bacterial infection in my throat area. Had I gone home without the antibiotics that day, I'm certain I would have gone back within a day or two, as the pain actually worsened on the first day of antibiotics. Then it finally started easing up. This is a perfect example where one word, fever, made all the difference in the treatment prescribed. How often do we go to doctors for help about our back and don't give them that one piece of information that would change the treatment plan in a major way? This is the type of insight and prompting the Holy Spirit will provide if you are open to it.

Physicians, doctors, chiropractors and physical therapists help us by applying their education and experience to the situation at hand. But they are finite and human. When you see medical practitioners, you do not know what state of mind they are in or what knowledge they have or don't have. Will you give them the correct information they need at the right time so they can give you the advice you need? There is no way for any one medical professional to know exactly everything going on with you because most of the time you don't even know what to tell her or him at the right time.

Quieting your mind and letting the Holy Spirit guide you can alter treatment plans and prescriptions and thus speed healing. The Holy Spirit may also help you in a chance conversation with someone who had or has the issue you have. Or the Holy Spirit may direct you to do a Google search to get you to the right information. In the process you might realize that you are causing a problem that doctors or medications will not solve—spoken by someone with a lot of experience! So yes, pray and trust in God for an instant healing because He is still in the miracle business. But also pray for the Holy Spirit to direct you to wisdom when the situation may be fixable with the right information, and pray for endurance when the illness or difficulty lingers.

I believe if you ask God for wisdom and are open to His response, your medical visits will start being more efficient and productive. You will start remembering things you need to tell the medical health practitioner, and he or she will be able to provide a better treatment plan. Or maybe your prayer will help the professional remember a situation similar to yours and what did and didn't help. Your time in the office should be a useful dialogue, as you have the right and responsibility to own your health. Be open and attentive to where the Holy Spirit will direct you for help. Even if you are pointed to something that seems as if it can't possibly help, try it. It may be the little thing that changes the whole situation.

## Believe God Will Help You

Matthew 8:1-4

*When Jesus came down from the mountainside, large crowds followed him. A man with leprosy came and knelt before him and said, "Lord, if you are willing, you can make me clean."*

*Jesus reached out his hand and touched the man. "I am willing," he said. "Be clean!" Immediately he was cleansed of his leprosy. Then Jesus said to him, "See that you don't tell anyone. But go, show yourself to the priest and offer the gift Moses commanded, as a testimony to them."*

The man with leprosy said something unusual: "Lord, if you are willing, you can make me clean." There was no doubt in his mind that Jesus could heal him. But would he? That was the real question. Do you believe God still heals people today? And if you believe that, do you believe He will heal you?

I asked a friend to pray for me and was stunned when she prayed for healing from my head to my toes. I had only told her about my back issues, even though I was dealing with health issues literally from head to toe. It was surreal. Yet it reminded me that God moves in his people so they know what to pray for on your behalf even before you ask and tell them. In addition, she sent me a wonderful note about healing, reinforcing the notion that God heals regardless of the "why." In the note she asked: "Are you willing to receive His healing?" I recall thinking, "Are you crazy? Of course I am willing to receive healing immediately!" But the more I thought about it, she was right. I didn't really believe God would heal me. I believed God could heal others, but I didn't believe it for myself. Nor had I sought God in this way other than just out of pure desperation. She said that healing takes no more faith than receiving the free gift of salvation. She talked about being in God's love and encouraged me to delight myself in His love for me. She said she would pray that I would not only receive His love for me but "receive" his healing. And in a P.S. she wrote:

*"You could pray that I [Tammi] hear and obey God, choosing not to do my own thing and that I [Tammi] fall deeper in love with Him."*

She reminded me that rather than spin my wheels trying to figure it all out, I needed to abide in Him, in His love for me, and let Him guide me step by step— and even when there is no sign of relief to believe He will make the way.

I began the journey of first acknowledging that God still heals today. I have heard of many miraculous healings in our time, so I know God is still in the miracle business. Once I convinced myself that God still heals today, I had to address my own unbelief about whether He wanted to heal me. This was harder. I prayed and then waited.

At one point, in addition to back issues, I had four non-life threatening health issues unrelated to my back. Then a fifth one started, and I felt overwhelmed. I wasn't going to die from all these issues, but I felt like I was falling apart. My life became complicated in just managing my health. Some issues, like huge dandruff snowflakes falling from my head, were embarrassing while others, such as a cut toe, were painful. I sat on my bed and wanted to cry, but instead I began to laugh, saying to myself, "Okay, God, this is all in Your hands now, and I'm going to believe that You will help me through it." I felt this incredible peace, the peace that defies human logic, and went about the rest of my day in peace. When I told my mom about this, she looked puzzled, and maybe irritated, as she was distressed over my health problems. Sure enough, over time each health issue was resolved by the Holy Spirit leading me to gain wisdom for what to do.

What would have happened if I had given in to self pity? Would I still have been healed but had to wait longer for wisdom for healing? Would I have spent weeks in distress, crying and angry, only to realize the answers were coming regardless? Isn't it better to wait with peace in our heart than live in fear? When I look back now, it is so obvious that God was at work the whole time. And my faith in Him grew stronger. I thank God daily for His goodness to me and for helping me overcome that crippling fear of "What if?" When we put our hope in God, there is no such thing. There is only "Thank you and amen!"

The real question, again, is whether you believe God still heals and will heal <u>you</u> or give <u>you</u> wisdom. Do you believe this?

Get wisdom from the One who gives it freely, Jehovah-Rophe. Pray for wisdom to discern the imparting of the wisdom. Know that God loves you and wants to help you. And as my friend wrote to me, abide in His love, knowing He will take care of you.

## Next Steps:

1. Pray and believe that God will help you.
2. Cast all your health issues at God's feet, finding the peace that surpasses all understanding, and be open to the Holy Spirit's promptings.

## Prayer:

Father, help my unbelief that you will heal me, whether by instant miracle or wisdom over time. Help me rest in You through this journey and know that You love me and want to help me. Help me to be open to the wisdom You will send my way for how to manage my specific back issues. Help me to be open to the Holy Spirit at work in my life. Remind me that this book is just an example of how one person manages back issues with Your help. Some of the things suggested may work for me, but others may not. Help me to be attentive to what You would have me know for how to manage my back. In Jesus' precious name, Amen.

Chapter 3

# The ABCs

Hosea 4:6 *"...my people are destroyed from lack of knowledge."*

This verse refers to lack of knowledge of God, but I believe it also is a more general statement indicating that we often suffer needlessly in not having practical knowledge that is available. We tend to think that the ones with knowledge are the educated and sophisticated among us. I've learned that the one who has the knowledge is the one who seeks it—period! Having knowledge doesn't require going to college. Often we seek knowledge by going to experts, friends, books or the Internet. But though we search, we cannot find the information we need, or we get misinformation, which can be worse. When I was dealing with my back issues, I found that there were many people with different perspectives on what I should do. This was confusing and painful—until I started asking God for help. Truth be told, I was desperate and crying out to Him for help. Not only did He lead me to information, but I learned something crucial in my relationship with Him. Getting the right information requires that you ask God for His help, be open to how He might bring it your way and pursue it when He prods you in an unsuspected direction.

When you start having back issues, the first thing you need to do is get information. This chapter will try to provide information on who is who, what is what and what is your responsibility. This information is based on my layman's understanding and may not be technically correct. You may want to cross-check with trusted and unbiased medical professionals (if they exist), medical books, websites and or friends. I use the word "acute" often in this book, so let me start by defining what it means to me. When I use this word, I am referring to times when you are in a lot of pain. Some acute phases can last months. Some can last weeks. Some can last days or hours. These will go on until you get on the right program to deal with the issue. Whenever I use acute, it means something has happened in the spine that is causing a lot of pain at that moment.

## Which medical professionals deal with back problems?

<u>Primary Care Physician (aka medical doctor or("MD"))</u>: This is the person you go to when you are sick from a cold or other virus or some other cause. Your medical doctor is also where you start the process of finding out what is going on with your back. Doctors must meet the state's educational requirements (Ph.D.) and rotational experience to be certified by a state as a licensed Medical Doctor. They will ask questions and likely get an X-ray done. They typically won't order an MRI but will be willing to prescribe medications to reduce inflammation and pain. If their initial advice

doesn't help or you are in extreme pain, they will send you to a spine specialist for further assessment. If your primary care physician doesn't refer you to one, ask to be referred.

<u>Spine Specialist Medical Doctor ("SS MD")</u>: This is the person who specializes in treatments for back related issues. He or she goes through the same extensive educational programs and rotational training as a medical doctor and specializes in spine related issues. The exact title will likely vary from practice to practice. You would likely be referred to SS MD by MD. SS MDs can order MRIs, recommend physical therapy and be involved in any surgery decision. They may also do the surgery and can prescribe medications.

<u>Chiropractor</u>: This is the person with a degree and license in chiropractic medicine. The educational and rotational experience is comparable to a medical doctor. They must meet national standards to be certified. Chiropractors cannot prescribe medications nor do surgeries. They focus on finding the root causes of issues. If they believe a situation may require surgery or medications, they will send patients back to their MDs with some guidance. Chiropractors can do X-rays and may be able to order MRIs. This second part is a bit fuzzy to me, so it is important for you to ask. They will do adjustments, also known as "cracking your spine" in a good way. They may do special massage treatments and have lots of equipment to help with spine rehabilitation. They may recommend proper alignment positions, icing and /or heat, exercises and nutritional supplements.

<u>Naturopathic Doctor (aka homeopathic doctors)</u>: This is the person with an academic degree and license in

naturopathic medicine. Naturopaths try to find root causes of problems and then use supplements and dietary guidance to help resolve them. Some naturopathic doctors have medical degrees as well, so they can do physicals, pap smears and other procedures and prescribe medication. If naturopaths or homeopathic doctors don't have medical degrees, they should not be doing these things. They should have some official certification and state recognition. They will usually not be the ones to assess a back issue, but they may be able to help with pain management, diet and supplement recommendations to help reduce inflammation.

Physical Therapist: This is the person who has a academic degree in physical therapy. Typically physical therapists act on the direction of MDs or SS MDs. They will help you with exercises and rehabilitation after surgery. They often run group classes for people with back issues. They have equipment they can use in rehabilitation.

Kinesiologist: This is the person who has an academic degree in kinesiology, the study of the body with respect to movement. Kinesiologists may have physical therapy academic degrees and/or some form of trainer certification. They focus on posture in movement and provide exercise regimens to help ensure good alignment and good muscle development.

Trainer: This is the person who has some sort of certification in physical training. The skill level varies from simple to complex, depending on degree and experience. Trainers are good at helping you look fit but may not be well versed in the subtleties of back issues.

<u>Massage Therapist</u>: This is the person who is trained and certified to perform various types of massages. The skill level will vary. Typically message therapists know how to do specific types of massages, such as Swedish massages. Some take more free-form approaches depending on training and experience. Unless they are working with doctors or chiropractors, massage therapists usually will have limited knowledge of back issues.

<u>Back Specialist Massage Therapist</u>: This is the person with additional training and certification in techniques to help with severe back alignment issues. Back specialist massage therapists will be more free-form and may help with trouble shooting. Also, they will be more expensive than traditional massage therapists in your area.

After reading this list of medical professionals, you may be wondering, "Who should I go to for help first?" I'll provide some insights on this as you continue through this book. It is usually good to start with the MD and a chiropractor. Wherever you see seek help, you need to feel comfortable with the care provided. If you do not feel you are receiving proper care or given enough information or insight on your issues, you should try another medical professional. Try to go to medical professionals for whom you have been given a positive reference.

One of the men on my Ethiopia mission trip told me about his chiropractor and how he had vetted the guy before he went to him and why he liked him. I was not convinced at that time that I needed to see a chiropractor, but when I finally decided to go to one, I chose this man's chiropractor. I was immediately impressed and have been working with the chiropractor ever since. In addition, the chiropractor has referred me to other specialists who have been very good. Any time I have not been comfortable with a practitioner, I have discontinued working with him or her and looked for an alternative.

Next you may be asking, "How can I afford to see all these different professionals? Will my insurance cover any of this?" The key will be for you to target who to see when you need more information on or further help in a particular area. If you have a lot of information when you go to someone, you can minimize your visits and get the information and help you need sooner. Sometimes it will take multiple visits. You will need to prioritize based on your level of pain, time and financial means.

## What do I mean when I say back problems?

In this book I am talking about back problems caused by spinal disc issues. This condition is often diagnosed as degenerative disc disease. The first time I heard those words together, they sounded terrifying. The good news is that this condition should not be life threatening. It just means your discs are prone to drying out or decaying. The problem does not spread to other parts of your body like cancer. The bad news is that it can cause a lot of a pain in various parts of your body (called referral pain, to be discussed more later) and may be something you have to manage for the rest of your life.

So you can understand this better, I need to provide information about your spine. Since I'm not a medical professional, I can only describe this at a simplistic level. I will try to relay to you what is most important. If you want an exhaustive explanation of the back and back problems, you can refer to medical books and various websites. In the simplest form, the spine is made up of bones, discs and nerves. The nerves run from your brain down the spine to the tail bone, and parts of them run out through your arms and legs. The bones in your spine are classified into five groups (from top of the spine to the bottom): cervical vertebrae ("C"), thoracic vertebrae ("T"), lumbar vertebrae ("L"), the sacrum ("S") and coccygeal vertebrae. These last two make up what is often called the tail bone.

Most disc issues tend to be in the cervical and lumbar regions. If you have a disc issue in one of these areas, you will likely have one in the other as well. The lumbar region can have four, five or six bones. This can be confusing since some people don't know this. So when I say my herniated disc is the Lumbar6/Sacrum1 or L6/S1 area, some folks will try to correct me to L5/S1 or tell me I don't know what I am talking about. It just turns out that there is variety in the number of bones people have in their spines.

The discs are in the spaces between spine bones. For example, disc L5/S1 is the disc between the L5 and S1. I was once given a simple way to think of discs—they are like jelly donuts with no hole for the jelly to come out. When there is a hole in a disc, there is a problem. When your spine is in optimal form, the discs will be nice and plump, and the nerves will have enough space to run down your back without being pinched. You will be able to move this way and that without pain. When something is not right in the discs or the spinal column, then you start having problems.

I'm focusing on disc problems and related inflammation, and not bone fractures or bone spurs or accident related issues. The most common disc problems are bulging, herniated, slipped or "disappearing discs." A *bulging disc* is usually related to a disc flattening, which can be caused by drying or inflammation. The disc bulges out pinching nerves. A *herniated disc* is one with a hole or tear that allows the inside jelly like substance to come out. Both the disc's outer material and the jelly may press on the nerves. A *slipped disc* is one that has moved out of its normal position and is pressing against nerves. A *disappearing disc* is one that is drying out and decaying such that the bones above and below it may be fusing together. You can find pictures online of the various types of disc issues. All of these will cause the nerves to get pinched, and that is what causes pain. And because the spine needs to move, every step a person takes can cause additional pinching that triggers pain. The disc problems/nerve pinching will also cause areas of inflammation around the spine. The inflammation will not be something you can feel or see externally, it is a more subtle inflammation that occurs around/inside the spinal column area. You will just feel the resulting pain.

## What does back pain feel like?

Now this is the most interesting part about back pain—it is often not felt along the spine or even in your back area. Since a disc is somehow pinching nerves, the pain is felt along the nerve being pinched. The more severe the pinch, the farther out along a nerve the pain goes. In fact, if you have pain in a foot or hand, it usually means the inflammation or some other disc problem is very severe. If over time the pain starts moving closer to your spine, this may be an indication that the disc is healing or the situation is otherwise getting resolved.

The pain can feel like, well, pain. Or it can be tightness from muscle cramping, numbness, tingling— or my favorite, zapping. I can experience several types of pain in each episode, depending on which disc area is flaring up.

For lumbar related issues:

1) I may experience a zapping sensation, like an electric current, down my tailbone. It goes from top of my lumbar region (at my waist) down my tailbone and then starts again at the top of the lumbar region. Since nerves send a very low grade electrical current, this sensation makes sense.

2) I may get severe tightness around my back, along the spine.

3) I may have pain in my left foot. The cause is in my lumbar but the pain is felt in my left foot. This phenomenon is called referral pain. It feels like numbness or tingling and varies in intensity over time though the location of pain stays constant.

4) I may get extreme muscle tightness and pain behind my left knee or in my butt.

5) I'll get all kinds of weird zapping and pain from sitting too long. This is difficult to describe. It just doesn't feel right to keep sitting.

For cervical related issues:

1) I may get modest headaches or find I am clenching my teeth while sleeping. My muscles around my jawbone area will feel very very tight.
2) I may get severe tightness anywhere around my neck, making it painful to turn my head.
3) I may get severe tightness in my left shoulder region.
4) I may feel tightness and or numbness in various spots down my left arm.
5) I may get pain in my left hand, especially along my middle finger knuckle, and it feels like numbness.

As you learn about your back problems, you'll have your own list of pain feelings, and it is good to be aware of what they are. As you identify what the pain feeling is (zapping or tightness, say) and where it is, you'll begin having a plan for how to deal with it. For example, whenever I feel the pain on my left hand and particularly the middle finger knuckle, my first course of action is to begin looking for tightness up my arm to my neck and to self massage. Usually after I do this for a while, the pain will stop. If not, then I have the next set of things I'll do. This is discussed later in the chapter 8.

If you have a lower back problem, you will hear the term sciatic nerve. This large nerve runs from your lower back along the top of your buttock region and down your hip. It then spreads out to various areas along your leg to your foot. There is a nerve path down each leg. You can find diagrams of this online. The route the pain travels depends on where your sciatic nerve is pinched. You may feel tightness/pain at the top and a zapping pain traveling down the nerve.

## How are back problems diagnosed?

If you go to your MD, he or she will ask questions and usually do an X-ray. Typically the physician won't touch you. I'm guessing this is due to liability issues, though I never asked. An X-ray can show whether your spine is out of alignment from top to bottom and if any of your bones are too close together or tilted or if you have a bone spur issue. An X-ray will not tell you with certainty that you have a disc issue unless two bones are touching.

You have to get referred to a SS MD to get an MRI. This includes several pictures taken of your spine, but each is a two-dimensional representation only, not a three-dimensional image. There are standard MRIs and weight bearing MRIs. Whenever possible, get weight bearing, as this is showing the disc when it is supporting the back as opposed to when you are lying down and the disc is not under as much pressure.

I insisted on being referred to a SS MD so I could get an MRI. A SS MD will have you move in various ways to see if this triggers the pain. My SS MD had me do lots of stuff, but none of it set off pain. Usually, physical moves trigger disc issues, but of course I did not have a normal disc issue. The SS MD told me I didn't have a back issue. Even though my pain was extreme, he thought the cause was a muscle problem, and all I needed was proper rest. I insisted on getting an MRI. Honestly, the chiropractor had convinced me that we needed one so he could help rehabilitate my disc(s) properly. The SS MD finally agreed to the MRI. When the results were back, I received a phone message from the SS MD. I'll never forget it. It went something like the following:

*Ms. Smorynski, as we discussed, you do not currently have a back issue. Your MRI shows that your disc herniated sometime in the past.*

I don't know about you but because I was in pain, I considered the problem a current back issue and needed to do something to address it now. I picked up my MRI and reviewed it with the chiropractor. It clearly showed a herniated disc. Also, we saw pretty clearly that the discs above it didn't look healthy either.

Another clue we had was where and when I was experiencing pain. The chiropractor had two charts on this, one for the lumbar area and one for the cervical region. Where you feel the pain provides clues to which discs are involved. For example, I had pain going down my tailbone and down my leg in a pattern that suggested a low lumbar disc. I got pain whenever I was sitting and when I would stand up. This reinforced the impression that it was a disc low in my lumbar region, and the MRI confirmed that assessment. When I started having pain in my left hand middle finger, this pointed to a disc issue in my cervical area, around the C3, and my weight bearing MRI confirmed this.

You should not try to rehabilitate your discs without a proper diagnosis. Review X-ray(s) and MRI(s) with your medical professional and have him or her show you what is going on. You do not want to take a bad issue and make it worse by starting a program and not really knowing where or what the issue is. There are some things like walking and applying ice packs to the correct area that don't require a diagnosis to start getting relief, but I highly recommend that you get as much information as you can about your situation before you proceed with other treatments like exercise. Discuss treatment and exercise options with a medical professional.

## Why do I have a back issue?

In some cases a person who is not prone to back issues may have one caused by an accident. For people in this category, if you are able to rehabilitate it, you may never have another issue unless you get in another accident.

I would venture to guess that most of us with back problems are not in this group. The rest of us are prone to back issues due to heredity. An accident may just reveal the problem to us more quickly. Or, as in my case, it will become apparent in the aging process but has been there all the time. I always had terrible knots in my shoulder area. This was annoying but not too bad. In time I started having issues down my arm, and then I got diagnosed with cervical area disc issues. The knots were a clue about the condition of my discs, but I didn't know this, so I never did anything about it other than getting a massage occasionally.

Poor posture and excessive sitting are major causes of back problems. The chiropractor told me that they don't hear about a lot of back problems in areas like Africa, where people are walking and up right all the time. Many of us in the U.S. sit all day long, so we have more problems here.

## *What is my responsibility with dealing with my back problem?*

As you read through this book, you may become overwhelmed. There are many people to consult and much information to digest. Keep in mind three truths:

1. <u>You own your back problem</u>. When you visit with any medical professional, he or she will talk to you for a sliver of time and so have only a sliver of the information about your back problems. To be most effective, keep track of what is going on and what you are doing and what you have told various practitioners. You cannot rely on one person to solve the problems you will face. Don't be afraid to seek advice, but ultimately, you will need to manage and own your back problem.

2. <u>You and your back problem are unique</u>. I will share with you what I have learned, which may not work for you. You can see what I learned and did and then decide what you need to do. You may have to try a few things before you figure out the magic combination for you.

3. <u>There is no one-time fix</u>. When you have your first back issue, it is very unlikely that it will be your last. I too often hear people say:

    *I tried this and it worked for a while. Then I stopped and my back issue came back. I guess that thing didn't really work.*

    I'm like, are you serious? You cannot spend three months strengthening your core muscles— those around your torso core and spine—and then sit back the next three months and think they'll stay that way. You have to keep exercising. You have to put in place a program that is multi-faceted and work that program for as long as you are able. There will be times when you are in an acute phase and you have to do more and other times when you're doing fine but still need to do maintenance. The key is that if you do the program, you won't have to give up all the other activities you enjoy, and you will reduce the amount of pain you have to endure over time and optimize your visits to the various specialists.

Whenever I read through the three points made above, I keep thinking, over and over, this is impossible. And then I remind myself to ask God continually for help and wisdom, knowing that with Him I can manage my back issues. In times when you feel overwhelmed, you may find it helpful to recite these verses:

Matthew 19:26: *Jesus looked at them and said, "With man this is impossible, but with God all things are possible."*

Mark 10:27: *Jesus looked at them and said, "With man this is impossible, but not with God; all things are possible with God."*

Luke 18:27: *Jesus replied, "What is impossible with man is possible with God."*

## Medical Profession Tension

Doctors are trained to diagnose and treat the pain point. Unfortunately, many have not been incentivized to solve the problem. Unlike in the old days when a doctor knew your name, saw you around town and followed your situation over long periods of time, we now have managed care with prescribed guidelines set by medical insurance. I like to call it quick-service medicine. This makes it hard for doctors to troubleshoot your issue because if they go outside of the guidelines, you may end up with a very large medical bill. This is true whether it's a spine specialist or a dermatologist. Doctors want to help, but given the cost-benefit trade-offs they are dealing with and the way health care is done today, they are limited in time to help. Some doctors will be negative about chiropractors and naturopathic doctors. Some are more open-minded. Do not be surprised if you hear negative comments about chiropractic approaches from medical doctors. I have a few times.

Chiropractors tend to want to spend more time with you to troubleshoot. It is logical that they will learn the most by seeing you often over a short period of time and getting feedback on how things are going. This is how troubleshooting works. Some people worry that once they see a chiropractor that person will have them for life. The reality is that if you have a back issue, you will have to manage it for a lifetime. I like the idea of working with one person over time because he or she will know me and my situation, and will be sympathetic to what I have gone through. My chiropractor makes me aware of new approaches and treatments to try, and he encourages me on my journey. Find a trusted medical professional who can stay with you over the long haul. It may be a medical doctor or a chiropractor—just find someone so he or she, like my chiropractor, can get to know you and keep an eye out for new approaches that may help you.

## Next Steps:

1. Learn about the different medical professionals and get feedback from family and friends about doctors they have seen for back issues. The more you understand about the medical professionals you will deal with and your back situation, the better you will be able to facilitate the healing and rehabilitation process. Gain wisdom!
2. Educate yourself as much as you can before you see anyone and be part of the process of finding a plan for your situation. Do not rely on the medical professions solely to do all the work or you will be very disappointed and frustrated. Own your health!

## Prayer:

Father, this whole process is overwhelming. There is so much to learn and understand, and I'm not trained in medicine. I can't even spell all this stuff that I'm dealing with. Your Word says that if we ask for wisdom, You will generously supply it. So I'm asking for wisdom. Help me understand who I am talking to, how to explain what is happening in my body and where to go for answers. Help me own my health and recovery process. I praise You for answers that are on their way and the wisdom You so freely give. In Jesus' precious name, Amen.

# Chapter 4

# The Process

Mark 8: 22-26

*They came to Bethsaida, and some people brought a blind man and begged Jesus to touch him. He took the blind man by the hand and led him outside the village. When he had spit on the man's eyes and put his hands on him, Jesus asked, "Do you see anything?"*

*He looked up and said, "I see people; they look like trees walking around."*

*Once more Jesus put his hands on the man's eyes. Then his eyes were opened, his sight was restored, and he saw everything clearly. Jesus sent him home, saying, "Don't even go into the village."*

Mark 10:46-52

*Then they came to Jericho. As Jesus and his disciples, together with a large crowd, were leaving the city, a blind man, Bartimaeus (which means "son of Timaeus"), was sitting by the roadside begging. When he heard that it was Jesus of Nazareth, he began to shout, "Jesus, Son of David, have mercy on me!"*

*Many rebuked him and told him to be quiet, but he shouted all the more, "Son of David, have mercy on me!"*

*Jesus stopped and said, "Call him."*

*So they called to the blind man, "Cheer up! On your feet! He's calling you." Throwing his cloak aside, he jumped to his feet and came to Jesus.*

*"What do you want me to do for you?" Jesus asked him.*

*The blind man said, "Rabbi, I want to see."*

*"Go," said Jesus, "your faith has healed you." Immediately he received his sight and followed Jesus along the road.*

John 9: 1-7

*As he went along, he saw a man blind from birth. His disciples asked him, "Rabbi, who sinned, this man or his parents, that he was born blind?"*

*"Neither this man nor his parents sinned," said Jesus, "but this happened so that the works of God might be displayed in him. As long as it is day, we must do the works of him who sent me. Night is coming, when no one can work. While I am in the world, I am the light of the world."*

*After saying this, he spit on the ground, made some mud with the saliva, and put it on the man's eyes. "Go," he told him, "wash in the Pool of Siloam" (this word means "Sent"). So the man went and washed, and came home seeing.*

In these three passages Jesus healed three blind men, and each one was healed differently. If you think about it, they were probably blind for different reasons. One was blind from birth. So it is only logical that each would need to be healed individually. This is true for each of us as we deal with our back issues. The logical question is what will work for me? You may be overwhelmed by the prior chapter's list of medical professionals, thinking there is no way you can afford to get help. I wrote this book to help you minimize the number and duration of visits to professionals, thus letting you to take control of your back health. First, think of your back health in three distinct stages: diagnosis, healing/rehabilitation and maintenance.

## *Diagnosis*

When your back starts acting up, the first thing you might do is use ibuprofen, ice/heat or rest to address the issue. But when you are dealing with disc issues, this will get you only so far. You need to get a proper diagnosis, and this will require a visit to a SS MD or chiropractor. You will want to have an X-ray and an MRI done, and you should insist on seeing the images and being shown what is what. This will help you understand what is going on with your back. As noted in the previous chapter, your description of pain and the X-ray and MRI provide information about what is going on, but you need to monitor the situation to know for sure that the problem is just a disc issue. Once you have the diagnosis, you need to understand if you are in an acute phase or just dealing with a minor issue to understand if you need to focus on healing/rehabilitation or maintenance.

My neck and low back issues were diagnosed separately. That is, I first went to the MD about my lower back when I had pain there and eventually got an X-ray and MRI taken. Then about 12 months later when I started having severe pain issues in my left shoulder and arm, my chiropractor had me get an X-Ray and a weight bearing MRI taken on my neck area.

Since that initial diagnosis in each area, I have not had to get another X-ray or MRI because I now know what my back feels like when I'm having a flare-up, and I know what to do. I have thought about requesting updated MRIs on both areas to see if there is anything else I should be aware of, but since both areas have flared-up severely only once since the initial time, I have not done this so as to keep my costs down.

## *Healing/Rehabilitation*

If you are in an acute phase, your key focus will be on reducing inflammation and thereby reducing pain. You need to focus on healing and rehabilitation. See Chapters 5-8 for more information on this area. One item covered in Chapter 9 that should also be done during this time is walking at least 20 minutes a day. This will help your mood and muscle tone and keep your body moving. If walking is painful and you have access to a pool, then swim. Find some low-impact activity you can do during this period. You do not want to be stationary, as this is not good for your mental state or your back.

When my lower back first went out, I was in pain for long stretches every day. When I took medication, eventually replaced with supplements, it would numb the pain for a period of time, but I would be reminded by the increasing pain when it was time to take the next dose. Certain postures would cause additional pain. I recall asking my chiropractor if the pain would ever go away. He told me something like the following:

- Within each day, you'll start having periods of time with no pain.

- Then within a week, you'll have a whole day with no pain.
- Eventually it will be two pain free days and then three.
- Then you'll wake up one day and not even remember the last full day you had pain.
- You will go along with no pain and then something will flare-up. When it does, do not wait to deal with it, or it may put you back at the beginning of this cycle. Start dealing with it immediately.

## Maintenance

If you are coming out of an acute phase or currently having no back issues, then you need to concentrate on maintenance. This will include doing the healing and rehabilitation items discussed in Chapters 5-8 at less frequent intervals. Also, you will add exercises discussed in Chapter 9 to maintain your back and reduce chances of relapses. As mentioned often in this book, the reality is that disc issues are not a one-time event. They will be an ongoing health issue that you have to manage. The more proactive you are, the less costly it will be for you to manage over the long haul. You will have less pain and fewer restrictions in your lifestyle.

## Weather

Since my back first started having issues, I've noticed that it seems to act up the most during the late fall heading in to winter. The chiropractor said those in his profession see an increase in back-related office visits during this time. I don't know if it's temperature or air pressure changes or what, but this is usually the time of the year when I have to be more sensitive to how long I sit. Also, I need to pay attention to my posture, especially in my neck region. I do not take any anti-inflammatory medications or supplements, as I want to feel what is going on, and I adjust my posture or the intervals on activities like icing or traction—both discussed later in this book. If you are aware of how weather may impact your back, you can prepare and be attentive before your pain gets out of control.

It was fall when I started writing this book, and my back acted up—surprise, surprise! As usual, there was the immediate panic. Is this a severe situation or just a flare-up? It is quite overwhelming when it happens. As with all my health issues, I raised the subject of back pain in prayer and just knew that, no matter what, God would walk me through this series of issues. I immediately increased icing, took an anti-inflammatory on two separate days a few weeks apart, increased the frequency of using my neck traction device and watched how much sitting I did. I also paid attention to my posture. And, as has happened in the past five or six years, I found that the flare-up receded, especially as we headed into the new year. Thank God for seasonal changes!

## *Next Steps:*

1. Ensure that you have a proper diagnosis and understand what is happening in your body to cause the pain you feel.
2. Today, determine if you are in a severe acute phase or just a temporary flare-up.
3. Based on the diagnosis and the severity, decide what to focus on now versus later.

## *Prayer:*

Father, everyone is trying to give me advice for how to take care of my back, and I don't know what is right for my specific situation. However, I know that You know all things and that You care for me as a good father would want to help me if I asked. Help me have discernment and be patient to take things one day at a time. Your ways are far better than mine, so I will trust You to lead me. Thank you for opening my mind to what lies ahead and to the new things I will need to learn to do to manage my specific back issues and not rely solely on what worked for someone else. In Jesus' name, Amen.

Chapter 5

# Medications, Supplements and Surgery

1 Timothy 5:23

*"Stop drinking only water, and use a little wine because of your stomach and your frequent illness."*

Proverbs 20:1

*"Wine is a mocker and beer a brawler; whoever is led astray by them is not wise."*

In the first Scripture verse, Paul recommends that Timothy use a <u>small</u> dosage of wine to help a stomach issue. However, in the second verse we are reminded that when wine is consumed in excess, it can cause great heartache and enable someone to make bad decisions or be unwise. Medication too, when used properly, can help, but when it is used in excess, it can cause many problems.

## *Medications*

When you are in the acute phase, you need to reduce the inflammation in order to diminish pain. This is part of what allows your body to begin moving

59

toward a healing process. If you are panicking over the pain, it probably makes sense to see a MD who will prescribe muscle relaxers and pain killers and suggest over the counter anti-inflammatory drugs. Ask your physician to limit the prescriptions to a short period of time and then look to replace them with supplements and other forms of treatment described later.

I once heard a doctor say that any medication you take has a very small amount of poison in it. That is why there are side effects. This completely made sense to me. If a medication is poison-free, it would have no side effects. I was convinced early on that I did not want to be on medications, as I would be forever managing my back pain and the side effects of prescription drugs. The most severe side effect is addiction to the pain pills. We all probably know someone or have heard of someone addicted to pain pills, so let us not be one of them by using them on a limited basis whenever possible.

Doctors can do a shot in the spine. I've never done this, as it just sounds wrong to me. It does give you fast relief, but this lasts only for a while. If you aren't doing other things while the pain is temporarily gone, you will find that pain comes right back. Also, you will lose the sensitivity you need to avoid certain positions and so may inadvertently worsen the pain. For example, I had pain when I sat. If I had done the shot, I wouldn't have had pain when sitting, so I probably would have sat a lot. What I learned for my back issue is that avoiding sitting helped me get on the healing path. Everyone I know who had the shot was happy at first but then acknowledged the pain came back. Often they would consider asking for another shot. MDs won't do this very often, thankfully. Further, there may be side effect issues like a drying out of the discs or addiction to artificial pain relief.

Pain tells us something about our bodies. Several people have said I should consider acupuncture to get rid of my pain. However, as aforementioned, if I were to do this, I would sit more because I would not be motivated by the pain to avoid sitting. (I discuss this further in the Posture section.) My chiropractor says pain equals inflammation. So feeling some pain will remind me to avoid sitting, to ice and to take measures to help reduce the inflammation.

Most people think all ibuprofens are the same, but I have heard this is not quite true. Various brands of ibuprofen are similar but come in slightly different formulations. When my back first went out, I used one particular brand name ibuprofen and it worked great. During a second, lengthier episode, it gave me no relief. I was at my mom's house and ran out of that brand. We were on a tight schedule, I was in pain, and I needed to sit for an extended period of time to drive, so I asked my mom for whatever she had. She gave me a different brand name ibuprofen. I wasn't sure it would help much since at the same dosage level my original brand name ibuprofen wasn't helping much that day. I was stunned to find that I felt better immediately. Now if I need something when my lower back acts up, I'll try one particular brand first. I've since found that a different brand seems to work best for my neck flare-ups. Whenever I'm in an acute phase and want quick relief, I will try one for a day, and if I don't get relief, I'll try another brand or generics until I find one that seems to work best. Luckily, this has happened only a couple of times since the summer of 2007.

I have had family and friends also taking one of the ibuprofens with no relief, so I suggested they try another one. Since they had always used that brand, they were certain I was wrong and would resist my recommendation. I would end up buying them the other ones to get them to try them, and they would always be amazed that it did matter. It is so simple, but many people don't know this. Always take ibuprofen with food even if you have an iron stomach. When you are taking it over long periods of time, it can really wreak havoc on your stomach, and some believe this may be counterproductive, as it may dry out your discs. This could be an old wives' tale, but it makes sense to me since it is reducing inflammation somehow.

I did use one muscle relaxer at the beginning on a low dosage at night for about a month, if even that long. I have little knowledge of this topic, and I'm not sure the medication helped, as I still had discomfort when I slept.

### Supplements

Even better than medications are supplements and foods that reduce inflammation. Some MDs are open to this approach, but many are not, so beware. I wish that supplements did not have side effects, but they actually can if you have various type of allergies. I moved from a brand name ibuprofen to an anti-inflammatory supplement, taken without food, and found it worked well. The reason I know it worked, and not just because my back was better, is that while I was using it, I didn't have cramps and bloating during that time of the month. It seems to work better over longer use versus for quick relief. This supplement has pineapple, which is acidic. I'm unfortunately sensitive to acidic foods like oranges, pineapple and coffee so I have to be careful with them. My chiropractor recently told me about another anti-inflammatory supplement to try as a replacement since it doesn't have the acid issue. I don't know what is in it, but it seems to work too, and, like initial anti-inflammatory supplement, it works better over a longer period versus the ibuprofens. Consulting a chiropractor or naturopathic doctor would be a good idea if you have any allergies.

Fish oil is another way to reduce inflammation. You have to take a proper formulation. Some people might recommend shellfish based oil. I think I have a sensitivity to it so am avoiding it. There have been some cases of eczema being exacerbated when folks take a lot of fish oil. Again, consult a chiropractor or naturopathic doctor if you have any skin allergies and to ensure you are taking the proper formulation.

There are other supplements that I took the first couple of years. When I started having eczema for the first time in my life, I decided to get off all supplements to see if they were part of the issue. I have been doing fine without the supplements. If I did go into a very long acute phase, I would be open to going back on all of them.

If you can handle the acid, raw pineapple (1 hour before and 2 hours after eating) may be useful for you. Berries, berries and more berries may help. There are lots of foods that your chiropractor or naturopathic doctor can recommend or you can find online that may help. Besides, who wouldn't want to eat more berries!

Whether you are using an ibuprofen-based medication or supplements to reduce inflammation, there is a right way and a wrong way to take them. Many people take them when they feel pain, and then when they haven't felt pain in a while, they stop cold turkey. This is fine for a temporary flare-up. It is not so great when you are in a very acute phase that will take longer to get through. If you are new to having disc issues, you are better off tapering off the medications/supplements. When you take the medication, it begins reducing inflammation, but it is not totally gone just because you don't feel it. So if you stop taking it, then you will find in a couple of days the pain is back and you will be forced to start over in reducing the inflammation. If you taper down... say 2 pills 3x a day, then 2 pills 2x a day, then 1 pill 2x a day...you will notice as you ramp down on the pills that pain will continue to be gone, but you are also reducing the inflammation so that when you come off the pills, you shouldn't get a flare-up right away unless you do something that exacerbates your back or you are "just having bad luck with your back." [See Figure 2, not medically accurate, just for illustrative purposes only.]

The graph on the left is the stop and go. The red line is the pills you are taking. In this scenario, you take several and then just stop. Notice the blue line, the inflammation, hasn't had enough time to go down

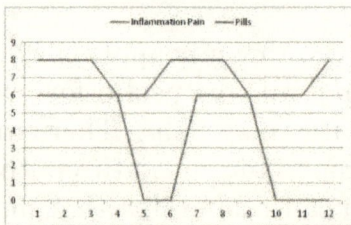

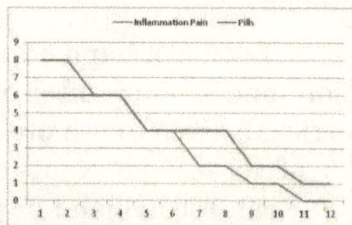

**Figure 2 - Inflammation Charts**

so when you stop, the inflammation flares back up. You are then forced to take the same dosage to try to get the inflammation (e.g. pain) down.

The graph on the right is the tapering down of pills (red line). You can see the inflammation slowly going down as well. Now if you stop taking them toward the end, the inflammation may not be completely gone but it will take a while before it gets back to a pain threshold.

My chiropractor would say if you feel pain, you likely have inflammation. Therefore, it is important to manage the inflammation all the way down and not end up on a roller coaster ride that will drive you and everyone around you nuts.

## Surgery

Another thing that MDs can do is surgery. I personally was not comfortable with this. First, it will cause scar tissue, which will create pain post surgery, and this can take a while to work itself out, especially if I waited for the scar tissue to work its way out naturally. Second, I didn't want to remove a disc or fuse bones if I didn't have to, but rather I wanted to try to rehabilitate my spine naturally. Any change you make in your spinal column will just put more pressure on the rest of the discs in your spine. Third, I still haven't met anyone who had surgery who has magically been pain free the rest of his or her life. In fact, it has been the opposite. People got temporary pain relief, and then things got worse as pressure now intensified on the rest of the discs and there was a loss of movement. And once you do the surgery, it is impossible to go back to the beginning.

Now don't get me wrong. I had knee surgery to remove stuff in my knee area, and it has been fantastic. Knee surgery and heart surgery and many other surgeries have had many successes for many patients over the years. However, surgery has not been shown to be a good option for disc issues, at least not yet. Of course, there are probably people who have had it done and it worked for them. But make sure you get all the details on what was wrong and what was done and compare that to what your situation and surgery would be before you use that as proof you should do it. If you are considering surgery, make sure you know exactly what it will do and what the long term repercussions will be. I'm stunned when I meet people who had back surgery to remove a disc and fuse two spine bones, not knowing that this would negatively impact the rest of their spine. If you have bone spurs, you will need surgery, as I know of no other way to get rid of them but via surgery. So there are times for surgery, but I don't believe it is the best option when you are dealing with disc issues.

## Next Steps:

1. Learn about the different medications and supplements by talking to MDs, chiropractors and naturopathic doctors and by looking online and talking to friends.
2. Have a medication and supplement plan for what you'll do to reduce inflammation when you get in to an acute phase and then manage your medications/supplements down over time.

## Prayer:

Father, I'm in pain. Please give me wisdom so I can receive temporary relief from the pain and begin to develop a lifetime program to minimize pain over the long haul. Help me to take only what medication or supplements are needed for the right duration and to taper them appropriately. Help me to avoid reliance on medications and supplements when there are alternatives with fewer or no side effects. You knitted me together in my mother's womb and know how wonderfully I am made. You created my body to be able to heal itself. You knew everything that would be coming my way and have made a way for me. I trust that You will point the way for relief. Thank you, Father, Jehovah-Rophe. In Jesus precious name. Amen.

**Chapter 6**

# Posture

John 5:5-15

*One who was there had been an invalid for thirty-eight years. When Jesus saw him lying there and learned that he had been in this condition for a long time, he asked him, "Do you want to get well?" "Sir," the invalid replied, "I have no one to help me into the pool when the water is stirred. While I am trying to get in, someone else goes down ahead of me." Then Jesus said to him, "Get up! Pick up your mat and walk." At once the man was cured; he picked up his mat and walked.*

*The day on which this took place was a Sabbath, and so the Jewish leaders said to the man who had been healed, "It is the Sabbath; the law forbids you to carry your mat." But he replied, "The man who made me well said to me, 'Pick up your mat and walk.'" So they asked him, "Who is this fellow who told you to pick it up and walk?" The man who was healed had no idea who it was, for Jesus had slipped away into the crowd that was there.*

*Later Jesus found him at the temple and said to him, "See, you are well again. Stop sinning or something worse may happen to you." The man went away and told the Jewish leaders that it was Jesus who had made him well.*

Many sermons and books have dealt with the above scripture. As I began this journey of writing, I started paying even more attention to all the scripture on healing, and something jumped out at me when I read these verses again. First, the man did not ask for healing. Yes, he was lying by a pool hoping to be able to get healed, but he did not call out to Jesus. Second, he did not know who Jesus was. Otherwise, he would have called out to him specifically for help. And yet, he was given information and followed it and was healed. Third, Jesus later let him know who he was and warned him that if he kept sinning—doing things he should not be doing— that that his situation could get worse. We don't know what the sin was or what "worse" might be.

I have always believed that only those that knew Jesus and believed him for healing could receive a miracle healing. God's ways are not our ways, and we need to be mindful of this, especially as we seek God for healing and wisdom and endurance. The outcome or answers to prayer may not come in the way we expect and may require us to change a long standing habit.

When I visited the kinesiologist, he had me stand straight against a wall. He explained that when you are in the neutral position, your head, shoulders, buttocks and heels will be against the wall, but your neck and lumbar will not. If you find it hard to stand this way, you will likely need exercises and stretches to help you so it becomes more natural. When you have an acute disc issue, you always need to find the standing, sitting and lying position closest to a neutral back position, where there is no pain. This allows your body to minimize pressure on your disc, and this will enable your body to reduce inflammation in the disc and thus relieve pinching of the nerves.

The following information on posture ideas is specific to my disc issues. That is, I have pain when sitting and when my head is tilted forward. A colleague of mine had a disc herniated around the same time as I did, and he would have pain when walking but felt fine when sitting. We sat next to each other and marveled at the timing of our back problems and how different our issues were but how similar the pain was. Hopefully, by seeing what adjustments I made, you may be able to figure out what adjustments you need to make for your situation. The key is to find positions in which you do not "trigger" pain. These I am presenting may or may not work for you, so get guidance and try things out to see what works for you.

## *Standing*

When my pain was at its worst, sitting was almost unbearable. The chiropractor told me to avoid sitting for a couple of months. I remember thinking, "You have got to be kidding!" Who can survive in America without sitting? We sit when we eat. We sit when we drive. Many of us sit at work. Heck, we even sit at church. Every time I sat for even a few minutes, I would be in so much pain, especially when I would stand up, as a surging pain would shoot down my tail. I thought I might as well stand.

If you do not normally stand all day, especially in one position, it is a rough adjustment. I would take breaks during the day and lie down, which worked well at first since I was at home and needed to do heat/ice treatments (more on this later). Another way to get a break from standing is to take a walk. I know it seems strange that walking would make you feel better, but it does. Any motion is better than just standing still.

I learned how to eat standing, read my Bible standing, work standing and even attend church standing in the back. This was very tiring. I would stand in meetings at work. I still remember standing in a meeting when a senior person in our group, thinking I was doing it to be cocky, told me, in front of everyone, to sit down. I politely explained I had a herniated disc and that my doctor told me to stand as much as possible. I figured it was not worth saying a chiropractor told me this—in case the senior person was not a fan of them. After that, I started telling people in meetings that I had a bad back and might stand at times to relieve back pain. I was surprised as often others in the room would say they too had a bad back and might join me. Telling people ahead of time made it less awkward if I stood during a meeting. One time at church, I lay down in a back row to rest while listening to the sermon, and a woman told me it was inappropriate for me to sleep in church. My mom jumped to my defense and told the woman I had a bad back. She said, "Oh, okay." I almost laughed because over the years I've seen plenty of people sleeping in church while sitting up.

I wore flat comfortable shoes because who the heck can stand in heels for eight hours? Thankfully, when I'm not in the acute phase, I can still wear high heels. I asked my manager to let me work from home four days a week so I could avoid driving in rush hour traffic and could lie down periodically to rest or do my ice/heat routine. When you have the issue I had, sitting for an hour in rush hour traffic is worse than going to the dentist! My manager agreed to this as long as I kept up with the work. If I didn't, we would discuss my taking a disability leave until my physical situation improved. Thankfully, my job is something I can do remotely for a few months. As I got better, I started getting in to the office two days a week, then three and then back to my normal routine.

I avoided flying during this acute phase. My company wanted me to travel to one meeting, so I got approval for a business class ticket by providing a note from the chiropractor about my need to avoid sitting. If our family went out to dinner, I would want to go only if there were tables where I could stand, and, luckily, many places have tall tables in the bar areas. My family, friends, co-workers and people I work with outside of my company were very accommodating. Everyone knows someone with back issues.

I had to get a standing desk at work. As my back healed, I could sit but knew I needed to stand more. I initially changed my home sitting desk in to a standing station by using books, a bed tray and a small night stand. This was not great, as I could not sit in this arrangement without changing my desk back to a sitting station. I found a bar stool to use when I was tired, but this was a not ideal because now I was leaning forward and extending my arms to reach my computer. You don't want to have your arms extended, as they will get tired. I eventually got a sit/stand desk for my house. These are not cheap, but for me this has been worth every penny. My back usually lets me know when I've been sitting too long, and I'll switch to standing, usually making the switch once or twice a day. When I had my second acute episode, the pain was a great motivator for me to stand while working.

When you are standing and walking, you will want to hold your head and shoulders back, your chest up (think of it as reaching your chest to the sky) and your lumbar curved. This felt awkward at first and seemed a bit pretentious, but nobody seemed to notice, and it helped. Normally when I jogged, I would do so with my hands facing down. This caused my shoulders to roll downward, which is not ideal. I had to learn to pull my shoulders back and keep my hands such that my thumbs were up and my pinkies down. This is still a constant struggle. I remind myself by allowing my hands to go by my hips from time to time. If my hands are palm down, I hit myself. This creates an incentive to get it right.

## Sitting

When my back first went out, I was driving a VW Jetta. I had been looking to buy a new car for several years, but could not make up my mind between a convertible and a mini-SUV. My friends thought I was crazy for taking so long to decide. I now see it as the Holy Spirit delaying the decision because once my back went out, it was very clear which to get. Every time I would get out of my Jetta, I would get searing pain down my leg. I had to drive my nieces somewhere in a minivan and found that I didn't get the severe pain when I got out of that vehicle — and could actually get to a no pain sitting position when I tilted the seat back. It was now clear that I needed to replace my Jetta with a mini-SUV since the seat height and angle are comparable to that of the minivan. If you can't change your car, at least tilt back the seat some.

This position does require you move the seat forward so you can reach the steering wheel, and your knees will be very close to the dash. Also, you will have to make sure to keep your head back. This sitting position will cause a lot of interesting discussions among your family, friends and co-workers, but it really does help. [See Figure 3ab.] It sounds like a lot of hassle to adjust to this new sitting position in the car, I realize, but the long term benefits are less pain and fewer problems later.

Figure 3a - Old Driving Position

Figure 3b - New Driving Position

If you fly, you should get a pillow that you can put behind your lumbar area. The airplane seats put you in a rolled over position. This is terrible for your back. They usually don't consider a pillow hand luggage, so you can probably bring one without consequence. I also have a blow-up neck pillow because I hate it when I fall asleep and my head rolls forward. A neck pillow will keep your head upright when you are sleeping. If your neck area is inflamed, the pillow will not feel comfortable. Just remember to grab both pillows when you leave the plane!

Two people I know at work complained of getting headaches. One guy had rarely gotten them and was now getting them daily. I asked to see both of them at their desks and was able to identify the problem immediately. Both sat upright with their heads down so they could see their laptop screens. You see people at coffee shops sitting this way all the time. For every centimeter your head is forward off the optimal point, you are putting increasing strain on your spine and causing your muscles around your neck and shoulders to tighten. [See Figures 4ab.] I told them to get a

**Figure 4a - Bad Sitting Posture**

**Figure 4b- Revised Sitting Posture**

separate, higher screen, to try to sit in a more recumbent position, and look at the screen as if looking down their noses. I also told them about icing and massages, topics covered elsewhere in this book. Within a few days they both told me they were getting fewer and less severe headaches. You do need to make sure your screen is not too high because that will cause your eyes to dry out from limited blinking. This is a very tricky balance. Most companies will accommodate the second screen and sit/stand station since they don't want you to have "ergo issues" at work. If you are on your laptop only, try to be aware of your posture and head position and take breaks as well as ice. You should also consider getting massages.

## *Sleeping*

Finally, we cover my favorite posture subject, the sleeping position. I use to sleep like a princes—that is, head high on stack of pillows. This was terrible for my lower back. I didn't like sleeping flat because I would cough a lot.

When I was in a very acute phase of pain, the chiropractor recommended the following changes and suggested that I try not to sleep on my side till the pain subsided. It was very hard for me to stay on my back all night, but when you're in pain, you'll do it if it helps. I don't sleep on my stomach so have no suggestions to make on this.

First, I had to lie flat on my back – no more stack of pillows. I was very concerned about the coughing issue, but the chiropractor assured me that my neck pillow would help. This was a big change for me, and I wouldn't have gone through with it had I not been in such pain.

Second, specifically directed at my neck, he convinced me to get a memory foam type pillow with a roll on the front, which goes under your neck and keeps you looking at the ceiling! When I was in the acute neck phase, the pillow did cause pain because I had inflammation in my neck area. I did special neck exercises, iced and got massages and eventually was able to use the pillow. It was awkward at first, but now I'm used to it. In fact, I hate going anywhere without my pillow. When I travel and I can't take my pillow because I don't want to check luggage, I will pull the regular pillow in the hotel up under my neck as best as I can and let my head roll back over it. This is not perfect, but it is much more comfortable than allowing my head to roll forward.

Third, specifically directed at my lumbar region, the chiropractor had me put a pillow under my knees. This was awkward and hard to get used to at first, but, as with the neck pillow, I did get used to it. My nieces think I look silly when I get into bed. I just yawn, smile and go to sleep. [See Figures 5 & 6.] Bed types are covered later, in the Heat vs. Ice chapter.

Figure 5 - Pillow              Figure 6 - Pillow under knees

## *Other Posture-Related Items*

During my initial acute phase, a number of things became problematic. I delayed doing some things, I had to make some permanent adjustments and in some cases, and I had to suck it up and deal with the temporary pain caused by the situation.

Two areas in which I was *able to delay* doing things were shaving my legs and dealing with my toenails. I didn't shave for a while but eventually got my legs waxed. I don't really like doing this. I was so thrilled when I could finally shave my legs without pain! When I couldn't stand my toenails any longer, I found a lady who would give me pedicures while I was lying down. Although this is better than sitting, it is NOT relaxing! As my back improved, I found a nail salon that had chairs that reclined and pillows to put behind my back. That seemed to work. I can now do my own pedicures, but to ensure that I don't whack my back out, I do "minor maintenance" and visit the nail salon every six to eight weeks.

Three areas that I had to *change permanently* had to deal with my purse, swimwear and underwear. When my neck was having issues, the chiropractor told me I needed to stop using purses with straps that went around my neck. I had chosen this purse style when I lived in Washington D.C. and New York City, as I could easily keep purses in front of me and hold them so that they would be less likely to be swiped. Since I no longer live in a big city, I feel comfortable with purses that I can carry in my hand and periodically wear on my shoulder. I noticed a big difference when I switched. I tried going back when things calmed down, but my neck would immediately feel uncomfortable from the pressure on it. Swimwear presented a similar issue. During my nieces' annual summer visit, we went swimming, and I wore a suit that had a strap that went around my neck. Almost immediately I felt pain in my neck area. As the day wore on, I knew that I would be avoiding that type of swimwear.

Most surprisingly, there were also underwear issues. When my back first went out, I noticed that when I wore certain type of underwear, my back would feel more hyped up along the sciatic nerve path from my spine along my back and down by the glut area. I tried different types, and it became clear that certain kinds of underwear caused my sciatic nerve to become more active while others did not. Unfortunately, one that was ideal seemed to make me more prone to hemorrhoids, so I had to find an alternative that helped with one problem and did not cause the other. Thankfully, I did find a solution. As you adjust your clothing and accessory options, be on the watch for unintended consequences. Also, just because it worked for me does not mean it will be the right option for you. This is where "listening" to your body and the Holy Spirit's promptings will be important.

Two areas in which I had to *suck it up* were bathroom visits and putting on knee highs and socks. Since I'm a woman, bathroom visits were complete torture. I had to mentally prepare for the pain each time. I tried to be quick, but there are just times when you can't be. Interestingly, the reduction in pain during my bathroom visits helped me monitor the improvement in my back. I had a really tough time putting on socks. I tried standing and lying down, but it seemed fastest to put them on sitting and just manage through the pain. After my back got better, I saw in a catalog a device that helps people put on socks when they can't bend down. Had I known about this, I would have gotten it in a heartbeat. If I ever have pain putting on my socks again, I guarantee I'll be looking for that device.

For my job, I take a laptop back and forth to work. Before my back went out, I always used a backpack for my computer. I was very good about putting the backpack on completely and not just carrying it on one shoulder. It is still okay for me to do this. I used to use a brief case with a shoulder strap but stopped using it because it bothered my shoulder. I have considered using the kind of case that you role behind you. The big issue in this for me is that it causes me to walk with a slight twist. I didn't like the idea of this, so I just stuck with the backpack.

## Next Steps:

1. Get an initial assessment of your standing posture. Think through what simple adjustments you need to make in how you stand to be in a neutral position. Consider how this translates to sitting and lying down.

2. If you are in the acute phase, pay attention to when pain is triggered and consider what things you will need to do temporarily to help get out of the acute phase. You may need to adjust how you work, drive, sleep, etc.. Make others aware of your situation so they can accommodate these adjustments. Some changes will be temporary while others will be for life.

## Prayer:

Father, I'm grateful that I can still stand, walk, sit and lie down. Help me understand what I am doing that may be causing me pain. I have many habits around these activities that I may need to adjust temporarily or permanently. Help me make changes that are needed to improve my health. Remind me to seek You for wisdom on all these issues so I won't be sitting by the pool for years wondering when if I'll ever get healed. In Jesus' name, Amen.

## Chapter 7

# The Temperature Packs

**2 Kings 5:1, 11-14**

*Now Naaman was commander of the army of the king of Aram. He was a great man in the sight of his master and highly regarded, because through him the LORD had given victory to Aram. He was a valiant soldier, but he had leprosy.* ...

*But Naaman went away angry and said, "I thought that he [the Prophet Elisha – added by author] would surely come out to me and stand and call on the name of the LORD his God, wave his hand over the spot and cure me of my leprosy. Are not Abana and Pharpar, the rivers of Damascus, better than all the waters of Israel? Couldn't I wash in them and be cleansed?" So he turned and went off in a rage.*

*Naaman's servants went to him and said, "My father, if the prophet had told you to do some great thing, would you not have done it? How much more, then, when he tells you, 'Wash and be cleansed'!" So he went down and dipped himself in the Jordan seven times, as the man of God had told him, and his flesh was restored and became clean like that of a young boy.*

When we go to medical professionals for help, we want an easy, immediate, low-cost fix with no side effects. But often that is not practical or possible. And, like Naaman, we get frustrated and angry. Rather than do what we know we need to do, we'll pout or just push forward until we are back in an acute phase and then hurry back to a medical professional for a quick fix. However, as with Naaman, who had to humble himself and follow Elisha's directions, we need to learn to manage our health problems based on advice we receive and the experience we accumulate over time. When it comes to our backs, this is even truer: it won't be easy, it won't be immediate, it will cost money and time, and we may have to deal with ongoing issues for the rest of our lives.

One area of treatment people will start and then discontinue quickly is using heat and/or ice. It is inconvenient, and you can not immediately tell if it is helping. However, if you are wise, you can easily incorporate these steps in to your daily routine, and over time you will know that it is helping.

### Heat

When I had my initial back pain, I thought it would help to turn on the car seat warmer as I drove home. This felt great during the drive, but once I was in my home, my back started aching again. I took some Tylenol and went to bed. The next day, I turned on the car seat warmer on my drive to work. Again, I felt great, but once I got out of the car, I could hardly walk. I struggled through the day and by the end of it knew I needed help. I called the doctor's office to make an appointment and asked to speak to an advice nurse. I told her what had transpired, and she told me that when you have inflammation, you should not use heat for the first 24 to 48 hours. "Use ice instead," she said. Duh!

During the first couple of months of my initial back episode, my chiropractor had me using heat and ice three times a day. It would be 20 minutes of heat and then 20 minutes of ice. Since I was doing a lot of standing, I initially welcomed the 40 minutes of lying on my back. I would read till my arms got too tired and then listen to television. Over time these 40 minutes three times a day became tedious. The chiropractor said I should try to do it standing, so I began looking for heat and ice packs that were worn in a pouch with a Velcro attachment. These made the routine more tolerable.

I also went to the chiropractor's office to use their decompression machine for my back. When I was going fairly regularly, three times a week, I could do a modest warm-up and come out feeling great. When I started going only once a quarter, I had a tough time getting off the machine. I literally would roll off it hunched over, and it would take 20 to40 minutes before I could walk around easily. The chiropractor said he did not think I was warmed up enough before I went on the machine. Since it stretches you, I needed to make sure my back muscles were warmed up. Previously all I had done ahead of time was walk, as I was being lazy and didn't want to jog or go for longer walks. The chiropractor thought it might help me to use the car seat warmer on my way to his office to help keep my muscles warm. So I tried that.

That day, by the grace of God, due to some scheduling issues, they decided to have me see the chiropractor before doing the decompression session.

This is the only time I can remember seeing him before I got on the machine, even to this day. He began working on my back and noticed that the muscles were inflamed. He used the expression "gummy-like" and asked me what I did before I got there. I told him. From that day forward we believed that heat was not my friend, and I needed to be careful in using it. Now, to be clear, I have gone into a Jacuzzi after a day of skiing, and that has helped. So there are clearly times when heat will facilitate healing and relaxation, but for my back issues, it does not. Now I understand why they sell those mesh back supports, which allow air to flow between your seat and back. Clearly, someone else has figured this out. I still use my car seat warmers, very sparingly, first thing in the morning on my drive to work—just until the heater kicks in. If I feel my back warming up, I turn the heater off.

You have to be careful with heat in other areas—showering and sleeping. I know there is no way you are giving up hot showers. I thought the same thing. Then one day while in the shower I realized I was not helping my back. Facing away from the water, I had hot water flowing down my entire spine. I could face forward but don't like that as much. I started thinking about why I like hot showers, and I realized it is because I don't like being cold while taking a shower. My mom had been nagging me to get a small portable room heater to use in my bathroom. Whenever my nieces were in town, we would turn it on while they were taking a bath since they liked their bath water to be warm, not hot. So duh! I decided to get a room heater and give it a try. Since the room was warm, I didn't need to take a hot shower. I can't tell you for sure if this has made a difference in my spine and back, but I believe every little thing you can do to reduce back inflammation will help in the long run.

Now let's talk about sleeping. I was considering changing from a box spring and regular mattress to a memory foam mattress bed. A sales clerk said memory foam provides a cozy sleep because it captures and keeps body heat. Since I sleep on my back, I decided to stick with a standard box spring since it is not prone to capturing/keeping body heat. I don't know if this would cause a similar problem for you, but I want to highlight this for consideration. I use a memory foam pillow with no noticeable issues. You may find that a memory foam mattress works for you because of how it balances out the pressure points, but if heat is an issue, you may want to stick with a box spring.

In the winter I'm usually cold for an hour or two when I first go to bed. I decided to try a heated throw. At first I was sleeping on top of it. Again, as I became aware of my back's heat sensitivity, I realized this was not a good idea, so I began sleeping under it. Also, I got a throw with a three-hour shut-off timer so I wouldn't wake up in a sweat later.

If you and your medical professional believe you will benefit from heat, than utilize the advice I give in the next section, on ice, but apply it to heat. Do be mindful of how it impacts you and consider icing after you use it.

### *Ice*

We've covered the need to be careful with heat. Now let's discuss ice. There are three things that matter when icing: duration/frequency, location/ coverage and convenience factors.

On duration/frequency: At first I went overboard, using ice beyond 20 minutes more than a couple of times a day. When I asked my chiropractor about this, he got me on the right path. You don't want to ice for more than 20 minutes per session because you don't want to restrict blood flow. You want the ice to help reduce inflammation while allowing blood to flow naturally. If you are doing 20-minute sessions three times a day, that is probably good. Over- icing doesn't help. I've heard that some folks are told to do 10 minute sessions five times a day. I think that is also good. The key is ice to help but not cause problems. Most over-the-counter ice packs seem to last only about 20 minutes. So I don't find a need to watch a clock for 20 minutes sessions, though I would need to for 10-minute sessions. You do need to make sure ice packs stay cold long enough to be effective, so keep that in mind. If you use something like frozen peas or ice in a bag, you may want to time your sessions until you know how they work.

On location/coverage: Another key consideration is icing in the right location and with sufficient coverage. As mentioned earlier in this book, the pain associated with spine issues is usually referred out to limbs and not along the spine. "Then where should I ice?" you might ask. "If pain is behind my knee or along my forearm, should I ice there?" If you are certain the cause is a spine issue, the answer is no. If the pain is in your leg, you want to ice the lumbar section of your back and make sure to cover a good area both on the spine and across the lower back.

[See Figures 7abc.] If the pain is in your arm, then you want to ice your cervical area. Again, it is important to ice a large enough area to make a difference in reducing inflammation.

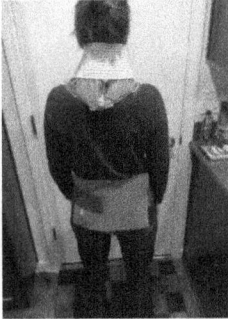

Figure 7a – Cervical and Lumbar Ice Pack Coverage

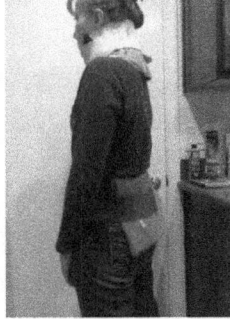

Figure 7b – Different Angle

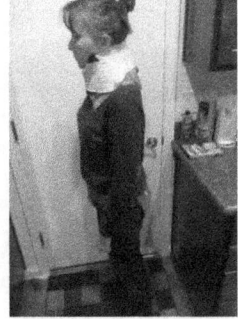

Figure 7c - Different Angle

On convenience: Once you have figured out the duration, frequency, location and coverage that works for you, the next step is to make it convenient so you actually will ice. Too many people feel icing is inconvenient. They don't do it until their pain is acute, and sometimes they don't ice then either. Icing is the cheapest and easiest thing we can do to help our backs. If you make icing convenient, you have a higher chance of following through with it. If you have to ice while sitting or lying down, you won't do it.

Get ice packs that you can "wear" and go about your daily activities. I like the neck ice pack shown on next page because it keeps a nice amount of cold for 20 minutes. However, it tends to leak within a month, so I wrap it in duct tape before I begin using it. This extends its life. I use a Velcro strap device to secure it around my neck. [See Figures 8abc on next page.]

**Figure 8a - Lumbar Ice Pack**

**Figure 8b - Neck Ice Pack with Duct Tape**

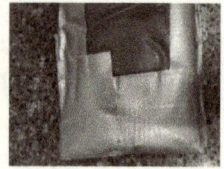

**Figure 8c- Neck Ice Pack – Up Close To Show Duct Tape**

When I was icing twice a day, I would take my morning shower, put the packs on and then finish getting ready for the day—put on mascara, do my hair, make my bed. In the evening I would put the packs on again and then go through my bedtime routine—brushing teeth, putting stuff away and so on. Since I knew my ice packs wouldn't last more than 20 minutes, I would do routine activities and then take off the packs when I was done. I'm sure there are times when I have had them on for 15 or 25 minutes, but it is okay. If you build icing in to your daily routine, you are more likely to do it. After eight years, I still ice at least once a day for 20 minutes. When I travel, I don't worry about it, but when I'm home, I look forward to it because it is soothing.

You do not want to put ice packs directly on your skin. I wear a thin turtleneck and pajama shorts or pants when I ice. This is more convenient than trying to secure and keep towels between the ice pack and my skin when I'm moving around.

If you are just beginning to ice and initially feel some pain related to icing (and not pressure or something else), I recommend that you raise this with your medical professional to get his or her advice. Some people have initial pain when icing, but if they keep it up, the pain eventually goes away, and icing will just feel nice. As noted elsewhere, pain is usually an indication of inflammation, and one of the best ways to reduce that is to do a regular icing program.

So even though icing isn't convenient or a fast fix, if it is done correctly, it is the cheapest no-side-effect way to reduce inflammation and keep it down. I have found that when I haven't iced for a few days, I look forward to icing because it makes my back feel better. Hopefully, you will find it helps you too.

One final comment on icing (and/or using heat), make sure to let your family members know about your plan to ice regularly. One evening while icing at my brother's house, my sister-in-law came home, saw me, dropped everything in her arms and sprinted to me. She thought I had been in some kind of an accident. This was touching, but I felt bad that for a few brief moments she was in complete panic for me. I guess it is nice to know how much she cares!

## Next Steps:

1. Determine whether heat helps you.
2. Get proper gear and plan to integrate heat and ice into daily life—more often when you are in acute pain and periodically when in maintenance mode.

## Prayer:

Father, forgive me for thinking I know the right way to do things and for my stubborn resistance to simple changes that will benefit me. Father, help me have discernment about advice I'm given on how to manage my back issues, especially regarding using heat and ice. Give me the endurance to do the things I need to do and make them a part of my daily life to ensure I'll do them regularly. Let me not focus on quick fixes but on new habits that will provide long term health benefits. Let me know when I need to humble myself as Naaman did to obtain the healing I desire. Thank You for making ice a part of this world so I can use it to reduce inflammation in my body. Help me be diligent in using it for that purpose. In Jesus' name, Amen.

Chapter 8

# Rehabilitation

Matthew 8:14-15

*When Jesus came into Peter's house, he saw Peter's mother-in-law lying in bed with a fever. He touched her hand and the fever left her, and she got up and began to wait on him.*

Often when we have a medical issue we think we are permanently changed and have to discontinue our prior activities. Jesus shows us over and over that when He heals, the person continues with his or her life as if the health problem never existed. He provides not partial or temporary healing but full healing.

Some believe that once a disc has herniated or dried out, there is nothing left to do but wait for the body to adjust to the situation or have surgery to remove the disc. Others, thankfully, believe you can rehabilitate your discs. My chiropractor is one of the latter, and as far as I can tell, he is right. The key is to do something to help with rehabilitation. If all you do is reduce inflammation and exercise, your body may recover slowly, but you can do other things to speed and enhance rehabilitation. These include adjustments, decompression, traction and other ideas as well as exercises discussed in the next chapter. And as you manage your back problems, you can continue to live a full life.

## *Adjustments*

Chiropractors use adjustments to help relieve tension and ensure that your joints stay loose. I call this cracking the spine and joints. I do not know how it works, but it somehow relieves pressure on the spine, and it makes me feel better. This effect is difficult for me to explain, but anyone who has had an adjustment will tell you it feels great, like a load literally taken off your back. Talk to a chiropractor about how this works and helps. People in this profession can do a much better job explaining it. Then you can to decide for yourself whether to try an adjustment.

## *Traction*

Chiropractors can "do traction" on your back. This is pulling your spine apart for a few seconds in the neck or lower back region. It takes pressure off the problem discs and may allow your discs to rebound or return to their correct position. Once you stand up and move around, the pressure on discs returns.

Some people use an "inversion table" to achieve the same effect, relieving pressure. As with all such devices, read the instructions and be careful. I have not used an inversion table, but I have friends who have and felt this helped them.

Decompression is another term you may hear that is usually associated with a traction device that enables you to stretch your spine and then release the stretching in a series of intervals. The traction reduces pressure on the disc and is believed to pull in fluids over time from the pump-like action. Chiropractic offices have high-end decompression machines that allow for different angles and time sequences. They are incredibly relaxing because you are strapped in, and the machine does all the work. You can read or sleep while in the device. The downside is expense, as traction involves trained personnel to assist you. It can be particularly expensive during acute phases, when you will want to go for several sessions a week.

To reduce costs, you might want to consider purchasing a device to use at home during the maintenance periods. They come in a range of prices. **You should have a proper diagnosis before you buy a home device to ensure that what you are doing will help you.** The most annoying part of a home device like this is that you must be actively involved in stretching and releasing your spine over a set period of time. Because you have to keep your eye on a clock, you can't relax. Also, the devices tend not to allow for different angles of pull and it is trickier to manage the sequence(s). You can find these devices on the Internet. There are both cervical and lumbar models. With some low-cost cervical traction devices you wrap something around your head. If you have the right shaped head, it may work for you. Not comfortable with that approach, I have opted for a more expensive device with a pump. You lie down in the device to use it. Since I use it almost every week, the cost per use is now less than $2 and going down, and since my device is still working, I continue to use it. One problem previously mentioned (the neck rash) is that I have found that the rubber parts on the neck piece chafe my skin. (It took me only three years to figure this out—it was only after many visits to a dermatologist that I really sought God for help!) I have since put a sock on each piece and no longer have chafing. The lumbar device I wanted required assistance getting in and out of, so instead I chose to visit my chiropractor for quarterly lumbar decompression sessions. Since making that decision I have seen a new device that seems easier to get in and out of, but I haven't bought it. You'll need to figure out what you are comfortable with and what fits in your budget.

My chiropractor has a vibrating neck traction device that was helpful for me when my neck was in the acute phase. It is hard to explain how it works, but I want you to be aware that it exists. Consult with a chiropractor to find out about this option, especially when you are in an acute phase.

When you are in acute pain, decompression will definitely speed up recovery and healing. Many people make the mistake of thinking they will be cured for life after going through a series of sessions, but this is not realistic. It is better to see decompression sessions as part of a regular back maintenance routine. I usually do a lumbar traction once a quarter at the chiropractor's office and use a neck traction unit at home weekly. It needs to be used in conjunction with all the other topics in this book.

Be sure to warm up thoroughly before using home devices or going on the machines at the chiropractor's office. When I went from using the lumbar device daily to weekly and then to monthly and quarterly, I noticed that I was having a harder time getting off the device—I literally had to roll off of it and stand up slowly. My chiropractor said I needed to do longer warm-ups when the frequency was only quarterly, as my body wasn't as conditioned for the stretching.

## Other Devices

New devices are continually appearing on the market and in chiropractors' offices. If you can afford to try different ones, go for it, but "let the buyer beware." If you can't afford all you might need, I suggest that you focus on decompression devices— stretch and release mechanisms—but remember that none of these provides a one-time fix. They all just help with rehabilitation and maintenance of your back.

## Massages

Who would not want an excuse to get a massage? It turns out that when you start having disc issues, your back likes to protect the spine by tightening up a lot. If a nerve is pinched, this will intensify the tightening, and pain will radiate down your arm or leg. You can use stretching to help, but without massages it will take longer to get your body to release the full tension. Massages done properly over regular intervals (every couple of days or weekly) will help even if you are not yet able to stretch. After every massage, make sure to drink water and ice the region that was massaged for 20 minutes. You may not notice a difference after the massage or even after the first couple of them, but keep at it. You will start noticing a difference.

You will need to find a massage therapist with expertise in spine-related tightness. Don't assume every practitioner can do this. Unfortunately, the good ones will be expensive. You want them to spend most of their time loosening up the areas causing most of the tightness, which typically are near the cervical or lumbar region. If you complain about pain in your hand or foot and the person is spending a lot of time massaging your hand or foot in the first session, he or she does not understand back issues, and you should find someone who does.

When I have tightness, tingling, numbing or "zapping" in my foot or hand, I will immediately start massaging my lower back along the sciatic nerve route (hip or glut area) or the neck and shoulder area. I try to find the tightness along the path back to my spine. (See Figure 9.) For example, if I have a numb feeling in my left middle finger knuckle, I start checking for tight points round my hand and wrist and then up my arm to my shoulder area and neck. I look for areas that are extremely tight. Then I begin working to loosen those, usually at the spot closest to the spine.

Figure 9 – Working from Finger to Neck

Then I work my way back down the limb. I don't wait around. I get right at it, knowing that the sooner I loosen things up, the better off I'll be.

I also usually make sure I have my head in a good posture. Often I will tilt it back for a few seconds. If that is not working, I make an appointment to see my back specialist massage therapist. I don't let a situation like this linger because it will worsen.

During an acute phase a good formula for massages is weekly visits with icing of major massaged areas after each visit. The massage therapist should keep notes on what he or she does each week to get the tightness down. If he or she is just "randomly doing stuff" with no clear plan for how this might help, you may want to switch to someone else. You should be able to discontinue your massage sessions for periods of time until your next flare-up. When I have a flare-up, which is rare, usually three visits spread out evenly over three weeks seem to be enough. You should notice improvement. Also, you need to be doing your regular maintenance routine of icing and exercise (discussed in next chapter). If you do not see improvement, then your issue is likely acute, and you should be visiting a chiropractor or medical doctor for additional guidance.

I'm often asked if the quick massages available in malls are useful. I have not tried them. For general maintenance of back health, I would guess they are. When you are in the acute phase and need specialized help, I doubt that they are all you need. Find a good back specialist massage therapist and just realize it won't be cheap.

## Other Techniques

There are probably many approaches that should be considered beyond what I have mentioned. Some that have worked for me are the Active Release Technique, the Elbow Technique and the Push-Pull Technique.

When my back issues started escalating, I went to a physical therapist who told me to do the "4" exercise (See Figure 10.) As I did it, I could feel that

**Figure 10 - 4 Exercise**

my gluts and hamstrings were very tight, so I worked hard to stretch them. Disc issues can make it difficult to distinguish a good stretch from a bad stretch. I inadvertently caused micro tears that created enormous pain when walking. So now I had issues sitting and trouble walking. If you are in an acute phase, be mindful when stretching and consider stopping until the situation calms down—in case you are putting yourself at risk. The potential for this is one reason I don't like to "hide" pain behind pills. When you are taking medication, you may feel as if everything is okay, do your exercises and inadvertently make your situation worse. Try to make sure you understand your current 'real pain' level and only do your exercises if there is no pain.

When I went to my first chiropractor appointment, I was in great pain. With a simple test he determined that I had micro tears in my left glut and hamstring. He had me lie on my back with my legs out flat. Then he asked me to raise my left leg and to stop when I felt pain. I could raise it only an inch or so before having to stop. He then had me roll on my side and used the Active Release Technique (ART) on my left glut and hamstring muscles. This is painful, as it breaks up scar tissue that has formed. [See http://www.activerelease.com/ for more information about this approach.] He had me roll back over on my back with my legs out straight and again asked me to lift my left leg till I felt pain. I was unsure but began to lift my leg. I was shocked when I was able to raise it almost 90 degrees with no pain. He told me to ice the area that evening and then to return for three ART sessions a week for three weeks. After the first week I was completely out of pain, but we continued the sessions to ensure that the tears were completely healed. Then we began troubleshooting on my back.

The chiropractor felt a lot of tightness along my spine, and I had a number of knots in my glut area. In the warm-up phases of each chiropractic session, his staff used the Elbow Technique—my name for it—on tight areas and knots. They didn't just jab my back but would place an elbow precisely at specific spots and lean in for 15 to 30 seconds. This hurt at first, but eventually the pain eased up and the area loosened. Over time the tightness diminished and the knots loosened.

I came up with the Push-Pull Technique. It is a variation of techniques I have done with the help of a spine specialist massage therapist. The goal is to generate muscle-activating resistance. At times when I play volleyball, my neck will act up from all the head turning. I have found that if I do a couple of things with my head, I can get my neck to calm down. I first tilt my head back and roll it from left to right and back for a few seconds. If that isn't enough, I'll place my fists on my forehead and push my head back with them while using my neck muscles to press my head forward. (See Figure 11.) I do this for five seconds a couple of times. I then will place my hands behind my head and pull forward with them as I try to move my head back using neck muscles. (See Figure 12.) I do this also for five seconds a couple of times. I have the impression that this activates muscles along my spine and secures

**Figure 11 - Fist Against Head**

**Figure 12 - Pulling Against Head**

the spine area better, but I don't know for sure. I do know that my neck area feels better and that if I do this, I'm able to keep playing.

These are a few of the measures I have found helpful. The principle involved in them is paying attention to what your body is telling you and doing things you know will help.

## Next Steps:

1. Learn about rehabilitation options by meeting with medical professionals and talking to friends.
2. Choose one or two to make part of your regular maintenance routine and know how to ramp up if you are in an acute phase. Don't let yourself stay in pain.

## Prayer:

Father, as You know, my diagnosis is degenerative disc disease, a condition that earthly wisdom says I will have to manage for the rest of my life. But Your Word says that with You all things are possible. So I know it is possible, even at my age, to be completely healed. Lord, I would like You to heal me.

I also know, from the writings of the apostle Paul, that at times You allow us to struggle with difficulties to humble us and teach us to rely on You. So Lord, if You choose not to heal me, help me to rest in the truth that You made my body capable of healing itself even as I age. Help me know what I should and shouldn't do to help my body heal itself or at least to minimize my pain. When my back hurts, encourage me to trust in You, realizing that the pain won't last forever and will settle down again. And when I enter an acute phase, help me stay calm in the knowledge that You have given me wisdom to take care of myself while the phase lasts. Thank You for all of the insight You have given me about managing my back. Thank you, Jesus! Amen

Chapter 9

# Exercise

Mark 2:3-12

*Some men came, bringing to him a paralyzed man, carried*
*by four of them. Since they could not get him to Jesus*
*because of the crowd, they made an opening in the roof*
*above Jesus by digging through it and then lowered the mat*
*the man was lying on. When Jesus saw their faith, he said*
*to the paralyzed man, "Son, your sins are forgiven."*

*Now some teachers of the law were sitting there, thinking*
*to themselves, "Why does this fellow talk like that? He's*
*blaspheming! Who can forgive sins but God alone?"*

*Immediately Jesus knew in his spirit that this was what*
*they were thinking in their hearts, and he said to them,*
*"Why are you thinking these things? Which is easier: to say*
*to this paralyzed man, 'Your sins are forgiven,' or to say,*
*'Get up, take your mat and walk'? But I want you to know*
*that the Son of Man has authority on earth to forgive sins."*
*So he said to the man, "I tell you, get up, take your mat and*
*go home." He got up, took his mat and walked out in full*
*view of them all. This amazed everyone and they praised*
*God, saying, "We have never seen anything like this!"*

    The friends in this passage of Scripture went
above and beyond. They not only brought their
paralyzed friend to Jesus but also opened the roof and

lowered their friend to Him. Often when we are dealing with a health issue, we try to deal with it alone. We may think: "I don't want to bother anyone" or "This is embarrassing." The reality is that it always helps to enlist family and friends to help you—within reason, of course.

On New Year's Eve many people resolve to exercise regularly and within three weeks find themselves curled up on their couches watching football games, eating chips and thinking, "I'll get to that gym next week." When it comes to back health, this is the surest way to ensure more flare-ups and pain. If you haven't been able to exercise motivated by staying in shape, you may not be motivated to exercise to stay out of pain either. If this is you, I recommend that you try ways to motivate yourself to exercise that have worked for others. Do each of the following until you find something that works.

- Join an exercise group—like yoga, palates or a running club—specifically designed for back issues.
- Have an accountability or workout partner.
- Set goals and measure against them. When you achieve one, reward yourself with your favorite dessert or find a website where you can get rewards like discounts or bragging rights.
- Participate in competitions that will encourage you to stay in shape. Local 5K and 10K runs are a good example.
- Participate in a sport that meets weekly. It can be anything like tennis or basketball or even tap dancing. Being fitter will help your back and get you closer to participating at the top of your game.

You do not have to be a pro. Find a group that matches your skill level.

- Prepare selections of your favorite music to listen to while working out or have your favorite pastors or television pundits on while you work out.

Find a way to exercise regularly, and you will be amazed at how you can minimize back flare-ups.

When I visited the chiropractor the first time, he was not sure if I had a disc issue, as he could not trigger reliable indicators by putting me through simple standard movements. I had an X-ray of my lumbar region but no MRI. My pain suggested torn muscles in my left glut and hamstring region. As mentioned previously, I had torn that area, so we focused there first. One thing the chiropractor told me to do was to stop all forms of exercise. Another was to avoid sitting. (I discussed sitting in the chapter on posture.) Though I do not necessarily enjoy working out, I do like all my extracurricular activities, like playing volleyball in sand and tap dancing. He said all of that was out. I know. You are thinking, "You just spent the last paragraph encouraging me to exercise, and now you are telling me you had to stop exercising?" Stay with me. The only exercise he wanted me to do until we got things under control was walking—lots of walking, which was tough given my muscle tears. Once my muscles were healed and walking wasn't an issue, we focused on further diagnosing my lumbar spine area.

During several of my walks, I noticed that my left leg would start tightening up at the end of my walk. This is odd since as you warm up, your legs should be loosening up, not tightening. When I told the chiropractor this, he was pretty sure it was a disc issue and recommended that I get an MRI to make sure he knew what he was dealing with so as not to make things worse. Once he saw the MRI and reviewed it with me, he told me to stick with walking but not do anything else, as he wanted time to get the disc issue under control by reducing inflammation and allowing the disc to heal.

As soon as the pain had come down, about three months later, we began discussing my workout options and restarting my hobbies. He suggested that I first see a kinesiologist at his office to help me put together a program tailored to my specific needs for stretching, strengthening and cardio.

## *Stretching*

I was sent to a group physical therapy session early on, and after one class the physical therapist told me to do the exercises and there was no need to come back. My disc issue at the time was very low in my back and did not flare-up when we did basic things like sit-ups or leg lifts. All the people in my class were really struggling with pain whereas I was not. It seemed as if nothing was wrong with me. The reality was that I did need help. Specifically, I needed exercises tuned for me and my condition. In a group session where everyone else can't do the basics without pain, the physical therapist will focus on them. I would recommend that you try to get one-on-one help for your specific body, physical shape and disc issues. Over time you can then join a group for encouragement and tweaking of technique.

My chiropractor sent me to a kinesiologist to get a posture assessment, and he immediately gave me stretches to start on. He wanted me to stretch out various areas specific to my posture issues. One area was my hip flexors. For most of the standard stretches, he wanted me to stretch after a warm-up period. However, he wanted me to use a foam roller before working out to stretch and work out knots in my muscles. [See Figure 13.] He explained that I could use the foam roller before doing any cardio activity.

**Figure 13 - Foam Roller**

He gave me exercises that focused on my gluts and around my legs as well as around my shoulder area. He emphasized that when stretching I needed to pay attention to pain signals and not push through as I had done before when I had torn stuff. Trust me, I have been very careful since then. Before you add the foam roller or any exercise equipment, consult a kinesiologist or trainer to understand which exercises are appropriate for your situation and how to do them properly. Many gyms have the needed workout equipment, and many devices can be purchased at sports activities stores fairly inexpensively.

As I began to do my various core exercises, I started getting a strange tightness or cinch in the middle of my back. The kinesiologist gave me stretches for it, the massage therapist worked on it, and the chiropractor team did the Elbow Technique mentioned in the last chapter, but the area seemed to be getting tighter, not looser. It was causing me discomfort even when I was standing. We were all confused by this. Around the same time I also began having issues with my neck. The chiropractor told me that about 70 or 80% of people with lumbar issues will also experience cervical issues. It makes sense. If your spine is messed up in the lumbar region, it will put added stress on the rest of the spine and thus impact the rest of your spine and vice versa.

In my job I meet many people in start-up companies, and as has been typical in this season of learning, God had a company come across my desk that had a product that can measure electrical activity in your muscles when you move. This is called Electromyography (EMG). This company's focus is on worker compensation claims. I contacted the founder and asked her if she could do an assessment on me to try to figure out why I was getting the cinch. I had her test my neck area and mid section. We learned two important things. When she tested my neck area, she determined that I only had one muscle doing all the work to turn my head. This actually made sense since the massage therapist had noticed that one section of my neck muscles always seemed inflamed and was larger than the rest. He did not feel the other muscles had atrophied. He just felt the notable size difference. When she assessed my mid section, she said the only muscles that were activating when I bent over were my gluts and hamstrings. My core wasn't doing anything. How could this be? I was very active with exercise, volleyball, tap dancing and skiing.

I provided this information to the chiropractor, and he altered my workout routine in two important ways. First, he had me get a head tension band and pull against it in eight directions.

[See Figure 14.] If I had any pain in any direction, I was not to pull in that direction until I could do so

**Figure 14 - Head Tension Band - Sideways**

without pain. This would help activate the different muscle groups in the neck to start working and better secure my spine. The first time I used the band, I was straining in most directions. One direction was painful, so I avoided it but would check each time if I could do that direction. Now I continue to do all eight directions and find it fairly easy. The massage therapist noticed a huge reduction in the inflammation on the right side of my neck.

Second, the chiropractor had me tell the kinesiologist about the core issue. The kinesiologist had me discontinue all my core exercises. Arrgghh! This felt like going backward again! Also, he had me start with diaphragmatic breathing. We all start breathing this way as babies. Check one out while it is sleeping, and you'll see its stomach going up and down. As we grow older, we move to shallow breathing in the chest. We don't know why we do this since it is not optimal. Singers are trained to use their diaphragms to breathe because they get the most air this way. I imagine major athletes are taught this as well. He had me do this for three weeks. I was like, "What! Breathing exercises for three weeks and nothing else?" Having just spent three months only walking, I was ecstatic when I got to add some exercises, and now those were being taken away for breathing exercises? And what about my stomach? Wasn't this exercise going to make my stomach stick out? This is not something any woman would intentionally want to have happen. He assured me that I would be happy with the results of focusing on diaphragmatic breathing. After three weeks, I could feel a difference in my core. At first my stomach did feel as if it was sticking out more, but over time, as my core muscles began to strengthen, I noticed that my stomach actually became firmer and started slimming up again. I then started back on my exercise program and could really feel a difference.

The first exercise he started me back on was a very simple one where you lie on your back, lift your legs into a bent position and then, while holding in your core, lift your knees to the ceiling such that your hips just come off the ground. (See Figures 15ab.) It seemed a bit ridiculous, as I barely felt anything

Figure 15a - Hip Exercise

Figure 15b - Hip Exercise (slight movement)

happening. I'm sure you are looking at both pictures saying, "I don't see any difference," but if you look carefully at the right bottom corner of the television set, you will see that there is a difference. I did feel as if it was stretching muscles around my tail bone area and strengthening that area as well. I noticed that the cinch in my back started loosening up, and eventually it went away. I still do this simple exercise to ensure that that the cinch doesn't come back. Once the tightness was completely gone, I added back all my other exercises. I also found that I didn't need to continue the basic breathing exercise, as I could feel my core actually working now.

Another exercise routine I was given for my neck involved a twisting warm-up activity, a pull/push activity on my head and then lying down for 20 minutes with pillows under my lumbar and neck area to help my body with the proper curvature. [See Figures 16ab.] The chiropractor also had a contraption you can put under your neck to help with neck

Figure 16a - Two Pillows

Figure 16b - Person on Two Pillows

curvature. I tried it out at his office but felt the pillow was sufficient for my neck issues. If you have a severe neck curvature issue, you should ask about the device. There are lots of options that a trainer/kinesiologist can direct you to consider based on your specific needs.

I was very nervous about bending forward since this had been a major pain area for me. When the kinesiologist saw me pick up something, he started laughing and asked me why I did the golf tilt to pick up the item. Honestly, this was another God moment. I told him I had been told to not bend down to get stuff. He asked me if I thought it was practical to go through life never leaning forward, and I said, "No, I'm sure I will do it at some point." He told me I should not be avoiding using any of my muscles indefinitely. I needed to be sure I was not in an acute phase and then, when I do things, do them properly so as to keep my muscles strong. So I began adding back stretches that included touching my fingers to my toes. I never realized how wonderful it would feel to be able to do that again without back pain! I am happily able to get my palms on the ground after a bit of stretching with no pain. And if I do feel pain, I know I'm in a flare-up situation, and I back off until I'm able to continue.

I found I had to do a few sessions on the same exercises. I would learn them in the first session, practice at home and then come back to have the kinesiologist see how well I was doing them and add more reps or give me harder ones to work on. For each new exercise he gave me, even though he gave me pictures and written descriptions, I somehow found a way to do them incorrectly until he corrected me a few times. And it really does matter that you do them properly. Make sure to go back periodically to have someone assess that you are doing the exercises correctly.

I haven't been to a training session in a while and hope I'm doing these exercises right. There are many stretches that should be considered in your exercise program. Do seek advice based on your posture and back issues. I know I feel more stretched out than before.

## *Strengthening*

The next area the kinesiologist focused on was strengthening muscles. Strengthening ensures that your muscles are holding your spine in the proper alignment. It also gets you using your muscles properly so you do not pull your spine out of alignment. In other words it maximizes the way your body was designed to work. He gave me a program that included sit-ups, leg lifts, a squat routine, front and side planks and a series of spinal muscle strengthening exercises.

For the sit-ups, the kinesiologist had me use an exercise ball. [See Figure 17.] He told me that you need to do both the crunch and an opposite move called

Figure 17 - Crunch on
Exercise Ball

the bridge to ensure optimal strength in the stomach area. I decided to add a side type crunch as part of my sit-up routine while on the ball, as in the past this seemed to help me in my stomach area.

This turned out to be a bad idea.  [See Figure 18.]

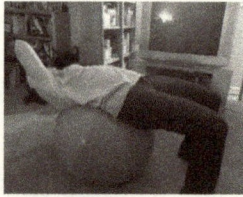

**Figure 18 - Side Crunch
on Exercise Ball (no-no
for me)**

When you are lying on your back on the ball and do crunches, you're head will go below your body. When you add side crunches, your head will do the same.  These moves done in the wrong sequence can dislodge particles in your inner ear, causing a type of vertigo.  I didn't know at first what was causing this sensation and had to work from home for a few weeks each time because the dizziness was overwhelming if I moved my head the wrong way.  I did go to an MD, but he told me to come back in a few weeks if this situation didn't improve.  Out of exasperation I went searching online for an answer and found a website describing this kind of vertigo and showing a rotational move to correct it.  After the third time of getting vertigo, it finally dawned on me that my crunch routine was almost the exact opposite movement of the rotational move that fixes it.  Now that I understood what was causing the vertigo, I altered my crunch routine and thanked God for not only leading me to a quick effective fix but also ensuring that I would not cause it to happen that way again.

For a set of leg lift type exercises the kinesiologist recommended I use an air pressure cuff to ensure I'm holding my stomach muscles at the proper tension for the exercises. [See Figures 19abc.] You place the cuff under your lumbar and pump the pressure to 40 in resting state. You then press your

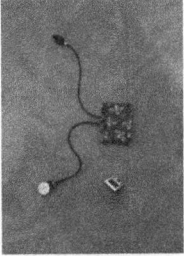

**Figure 19a - Air Pressure Cuff**

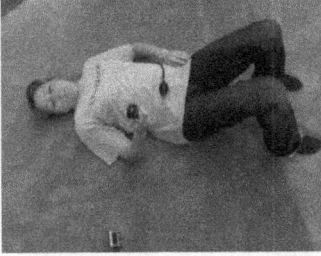

**Figure 19b - Set to 40 in neutral position**

**Figure 19c - Maintain 80 when exercising**

lumbar region down until the reading hits 80. Then, while doing the exercises, you keep it at 80. At first the needle will go haywire, but eventually you will be able to maintain a steady reading of 80. The blood pressure cuff can be bought at a medical store, a place where nurses get their outfits.

For squats the kinesiologist recommended both walking forward and side squats. I'm not a big fan of squats since they take work to do. At my prior church I was an usher and would help clean up at the end of worship services. When my back first went out, I was doing the golf tilt to pick up stuff in the pews. After my little chat with the kinesiologist, I began to squat down to pick things up or even bend over properly. Periodically, I would still use the golf tilt. After a few Sundays I noticed that my back felt a little bit better, but I didn't really know why. I assumed maybe God was being nice to me since I helped clean up His house.

I mentioned this to the chiropractor, and he postulated that the squatting was taking some pressure off discs in my lumbar region. After that I had a new found liking for squats. Now if I feel my lower back is acting up, I'll squat for a few moments for temporary relief. This is helpful, and I never miss doing squats in my exercise routine.

For planks the kinesiologist recommended the standard and the side approach. I found the standard plank really hard to do and very uncomfortable. You will literally break out sweating while you do these even though you are not moving. I took a group class for a few weeks so the kinesiologist could make sure I was doing both kinds of planks correctly. When I did my first standard plank, he touched my tummy area and said I needed to suck it up. I was giving it all I had, but my stomach was still hanging down. After the diaphragmatic breathing exercises, I could start to pull my stomach up. Now whenever I hear people talking about how fit they are, I ask them to do a plank. Without fail they cannot really pull their stomach up. If they can't do this, I let them know that they are mostly fit but really need to work on their core.

The kinesiologist had me do the side plank in stationary mode with a lift. Oh, my sides hurt just thinking about this! At first it felt like I was doing nothing, literally. So he had me do more. I still felt nothing. Finally, after I did a number of lifts, he indicated that this was enough. "Tomorrow you will better appreciate these," he said. I didn't believe him. But the next day I could hardly move. He was right. While it didn't feel like anything was happening, a lot was going on.

There are too many spine-specific exercises to go into them all here. One example is where you are on all fours and extend your right hand out and your left leg back and then hold the position for a few seconds. This activates muscles along your spine and holds things in place. When you are trying to build up your spine muscles, you will want to do a series of these types of exercises.

The key to strength training success is getting a good program that builds over time and making sure you do the exercises properly. If you can, you should enlist the help of a trainer or kinesiologist. Every time I was given a new exercise, it took at least one or two sessions before I was doing it correctly. If you can't afford a trainer, you can go online to find exercises and stretches. Get the instructions and have a friend check what you are doing compared to the instructions. It is important to do the exercises properly. Not exercising is bad. It is worse to exercise incorrectly and get no benefit.

As I was allowed to start adding back my hobbies, I noticed a huge improvement in my skills. I'm not sure anyone else noticed, but I felt an inner strength I had not felt before. So besides helping to minimize back issues, you may find you just feel better overall.

I've been told that several of my exercises are palate or yoga moves. These are both good exercise regimens to consider. Many people find them helpful. This may be another low cost option for you to learn how to do exercises properly and get motivated to do them.

## *Cardio*

The chiropractor wanted me to do cardio exercises three times a week. He explained that when you get your heart rate up, you generate endorphins. As we all know, these make you feel better. What I didn't know was that endorphins also help the body heal and reduce inflammation.

Up to then I had always used a stationary exercise bike. Since sitting is not good for me, we discussed using a recumbent bike. I was leery about this since it is still sitting, so he suggested that I try an elliptical machine. Unfortunately, that bothered my knees. So I decided to jog on a tread mill. That worked for a while, but then my hips and knees started bothering me from the static pattern. The chiropractor said this often happens when you do something repeatedly. He suggested jogging outside. I wasn't really keen on this. I thought about bad weather, the time commitment and the jarring of jogging on concrete. Once again God had to give me a helping a hand. My brother wanted my niece to jog for 10 days while she was visiting to help her keep in shape for basketball over the holidays. I didn't like the idea of her jogging by herself, so I went with her. It was really hard. It was surprisingly hard given that I had been jogging on a treadmill. I definitely felt like the tortoise and she was like the rabbit. I would remind her that I would finish before her by the end. Not! She still beat me to the door. The kinesiologist told me the treadmill does not give you the complete workout that jogging does. Boy was he right! After those 10 days I stayed with it and was jogging three times a week for 30 to 40 minutes each outing. (Don't ask me how far I go.) I mentioned to a colleague of mine that I had started jogging. He is a big-time jogger. He told me that if I jogged four times a week I would notice a big difference in my energy level. He was completely right. When I jogged just three times a week, it was a chore. Now that I jog at least four times a week, every time out is much easier, and I have the added benefit of reducing stress.

The stretching, strengthening and cardio routine I have may not work for you. The key is to get a program in which you can tell that things are getting better for you. Working out, whether it is following your own routine, attending a class or working one-on-one with a trainer, will go a long way in keeping your core strong and your spine muscles in optimal working order. It will also reduce back issues. Do not underestimate the value of a good exercise routine. If you find you start but drop out quickly, get an accountability partner, find tracking software online and get rewards. Or continually remind yourself that a little work now will mean less pain later. Do whatever you need to do to exercise regularly.

*Next Steps:*

1. Get a professional posture assessment to determine which stretching, strengthening and cardio exercises you should focus on first. Have someone assess that you are doing exercises properly. Modify your program over time as you improve your overall physical well being.
2. If you are not motivated to exercise, find a way to get that and then monitor how you are doing.

## *Prayer:*

Father, direct me to the right resources to get properly assessed and be given exercises appropriate for my situation. Help me release my old routine, how I thought I should take care of my physical health, and be amenable to a new way of doing things. Let me not do anything that will exacerbate my issues but only things that will move me in the right direction. Help me be motivated daily and weekly. You gave me an amazing body that can do many things. Help me to appreciate it and take care of it. Thank You for the people You have surrounded me with, who share my burdens and provide encouragement and accountability—and even work out with me. In Jesus' precious name, Amen.

# Chapter 10

# **Issues Not Addressed**

Proverbs 24:14

*Know also that wisdom is like honey for you: IF you find it, there is a future hope for you, and your hope will not be cut off.*

Proverbs reminds us over and over again how valuable gaining wisdom is. This book only covers a small portion of material on back problems and how people cope with them. There are a number of topics not covered because I have no direct experience with these topics. I want to at least mention them, however, so you can investigate them for your rehabilitation program. Hopefully, people who have experience with these topics will write helpful books about their experiences and share their wisdom to help others.

Acupuncture: This involves needles placed in particular spots on your body to help reduce pain. When I was in my initial acute phase, I was often asked if I had tried acupuncture. Early on I decided that I wanted to feel the pain I had to know how to deal with it. If I blocked or numbed it, I was not really dealing with the issue. In some cases acupuncture may be useful. Just don't chase it for the quick fix that may not last and will hide information you need for the long term.

Already had surgery:

This is a tough one and heartbreaking to me. A lady I know had two bones fused in her neck. Two years later she was in incredible pain and had headaches. The fused bones made it impossible for her to bend her neck as she once could, and other discs were now giving her issues. The doctors kept prescribing pain pills. Her insurance coverage was running out. She was unable to work. What made me angry was that they did not explain clearly to her the likely side effects of the surgery. When I told her what might be causing this new pain, she was dumbfounded. She didn't know that when they fused the bones that discs below and above the site and throughout her spine were now having to take on a heavier load and would likely start to have issues. Given the bone fusion, I don't know if she could do traction or if she would ever be out of pain.

If you have had some form of back surgery and still have problems, I recommend that you visit a chiropractor known for expertise in dealing with back and disc issues. It will likely be worth getting a second opinion as to whether anything can be done. At times chiropractors will say that there is not much they can do. They will likely make suggestions on how to alleviate the pain and reduce future problems, but they won't get you back to where you were before surgery.

Bones already fused: Sometimes a disc will dry out and disappear, and the bones above and below will begin to fuse on their own. I think this is rare but I am not sure. I would encourage you to get a lot more information on your options in this situation before deciding on any one path.

Disc slips completely out: A disc may slip out of its place in the spine if you are in an accident (such as being hit by a car), if you caused an accident (jumped in to bed in an awkward way, for example), or if the disc has dried out and simply moves. When a disc has left the region it should be in, the situation may require surgery and is beyond the scope of this book. If you are in any of these situations and the disc can put it back in place without surgery, I highly recommend that you opt for that and try rehabilitation. I would say this even if the disc is in bad shape. Having it removed and then putting in a man-made disc or fusing the bones will likely lead to other problems.

Shots in the spine: Some people in severe pain have received shots in the spine. This reduces inflammation and the resulting pain. I've heard that MDs can only do a few of these, so you should make sure you have tried every other option before requesting this. This is a temporary solution and will not resolve the long term issue of managing your back.

Spinal Stenosis: This is when the channel in the spine where the nerves go through is narrowed by changes in the spine bones. I used the term bone spurs in referring to this earlier in the book. This very may well require surgery and is beyond the scope of this book.

I suspect that many more relevant back pain topics are not covered in this book. If you have information to share about any topic covered in this book or subjects unrelated to non-disc back issues, please email me at EleanorPublishing@gmail.com.

*Next Steps:*

1. Talk to several friends and medical professionals about any item above that you may be dealing with. And do research. Get as much information as you can before you head down the next path. This will help you increase the prospects of long term healing versus seeking a temporary fix.
2. Share what you learn.

*Prayer:*

Father, I've read this book, got to this chapter and found no suggestions on what to do about my back issue. I'm overwhelmed. Help me get the information I need to understand exactly what I'm dealing with and make wise choices for the long term. Remind me that You knew about my back problem before I did, that You have a good plan for me and that You will be with me through this. I thank You for the wisdom and answers that are on their way. In Jesus' precious name, Amen.

## Chapter 11

# One Final Step

Proverbs 1:7 *The fear of the Lord is the beginning of knowledge, but fools despise wisdom and instruction.*

Proverbs 9:10 *The fear of the Lord is the beginning of wisdom, and knowledge of the Holy One is understanding.*

If you are a Christian saved by God's grace through Jesus Christ, you have probably begun to seek Him more fervently as you have read and mulled the prayers in this book—asking Him for guidance on your back issues and other health concerns. I hope this book has inspired you to seek Him first and let Him lead you to answers He has for you.

If you are not a follower of Christ, you can take advice I have given and try some of the treatments and exercises I have described. You might find help and relief from pain. If this happens, I will be happy for you. If you take measures suggested in this book and still do not get the help you need, I would encourage you to seek God earnestly for His help. You might think, "Well, I don't believe in God" or "I don't know if God would help me." Let me assure you that God loves you and wants only the best for you. However, a concern more important than physical health is spiritual well being—the need everyone has to be reconciled with God on this side of eternity. The first step on this journey is a simple one. You do not need to know everything to take this step. You just need to understand and accept the gift being offered to you in Christ. The Bible says that whoever calls on the name of Jesus and accepts His free gift will be saved and become a child of God. You may ask, "How do I do this?" The way is simple. Read the following statements, and if you believe them in your heart and state them aloud, you will be saved:

- I am a sinner.
- God sent His beloved son Jesus, who lived a sinless life, to die on the cross for my sins.
- On the third day Jesus rose from the dead and is now seated at the right hand of the Father.
- I understand and accept what Jesus did in love for me. I want Him to come into my heart and be my Lord and Savior.

If you have stated the above and mean it, you are born again. Receive God's forgiveness for your sins, His help in this life and a satisfying relationship with Him in all eternity. Get yourself into a Bible-based church, read the Bible and let me know about your decision at EleanorPublishing@gmail.com. Now you will really be on your journey to receiving God's love and guidance to improve your health.

Chapter 12

# Concluding Remarks

Proverbs 3:5-8

*Trust in the LORD with all your heart*
*and lean not on your own understanding;*
*In all your ways submit to him,*
*and he will make your paths straight.*
*Do not be wise in your own eyes;*
*fear the LORD and shun evil.*
*This will bring health to your body*
*and nourishment to your bones.*

Proverbs 3:5-6 is often quoted and memorized to remind us to trust in the Lord even when things do not make sense. As I began this journey looking for scripture on wisdom and healing, I was surprised as I read further on this proverb to find that it dealt with healing. It was a reminder that if we rely on ourselves alone to solve things, especially related to health, we will spin our wheels. But if we humble ourselves and seek wisdom from God, He will help bring healing to our body.

Wow! You stuck with it and made it to the end of my book. I hope you have a lot of good ideas for how to manage your back on an ongoing basis. I have included in Appendix A a sample worksheet you may want to use to consider what you will do in each of the areas covered in this book. I hope you are inspired to seek God for your own specific solutions. You may have wonderful insights of your own from your experience in managing back pain. Please write a book or email me at EleanorPublishing@gmail.com about what you have learned so I can share with others.

When my back first went out, I knew two other people who were also dealing with their first disc issues. One could sit but had a tough time walking. The other had a hard time standing but not sitting or walking. We each did different things in different ways. We compared notes and years later still compare notes on how things are going. The good news is that all of us are now further along and for the most part out of pain. We all have flare-ups at times, and we continue to manage them in our own ways. This shared experience has taught me that while there is no one right path in dealing with disc issues, I need to have a plan for addressing the challenges I face. The same is true of you.

No one should have to go bankrupt or live in pain. More and more information is available about what is going on in our bodies and how to rehabilitate them from injury or disease. You will need to learn about your specific diagnosis, put a maintenance program in place and ramp up the intervals when you feel you are moving into a phase of acute pain. You can manage your back to live a full life with a limited amount of pain and, even better, with no ongoing medications.

You can try to figure this out blindly or go to the One who knows you best, who created you and who has a plan to help you get through this difficulty. May I again encourage you to seek God for help? He will direct you to the right medical professionals, help you raise the right questions at the right time and provide wisdom to you and the professionals on what you need to do to minimize your pain and live the fullest life possible.

While writing this book I had several neck and lower back flare-ups. At times I felt totally overwhelmed, wondering if I was heading back to a long phase of acute pain and seriously asking myself if the ideas in this book would be useful to anyone including me. Then I would sit with God, allow Him to remind me that He is with me, seek His wisdom and remember things I knew I needed to do: increase icing, schedule weekly neck traction sessions, use the Push-Pull Technique and so on. I'm happy to report that all the things I did helped and that I have not gone back into a lengthy acute phase. I'm sitting—yes, sitting—at my desk typing out these final thoughts, amazed at where God has taken me on this journey.

I truly hope this book will inspire you to seek God first, receive His love and counsel and remember that He made our bodies with a built-in ability to heal itself. In other words, we are wonderfully and fearfully made!

# Appendix A:  Sample Worksheet

|  | Acute | Maintenance |
|---|---|---|
| Diagnosis | Lots of pain | Flare up, Irritation, None |
| Time Year |  | Pay attention during late fall/early winter |
| Medications | Ibuprofin - when most sever or seems like temporary flare up | |
| Supplements | Various - Use when need to reduce inflammation over longer period of time | |
| Posture | Mostly standing | Try to stand periodically |
| Heat | None | None |
| Ice | 2-3x day, every day | 1x day, when at home |
| Adjustments | 1-3x per week for 3-6 weeks | quarterly |
| Decompression | 1-3x per week for 3-6 weeks | quarterly |
| Traction - Lumbar | 1-3x per week for 3-6 weeks | quarterly |
| Traction - Cervical | 1-3x per week for 3-6 weeks | monthly |
| Massages | Once per week for 3 to 9 weeks | Flare up - once per week for 1-3 weeks |
| Stretching | Limited | Regular program |
| Strenthening | Limited | Regular program |
| Cardio | Regular program | Regular program |

# About the Author

Tammi E. Smorynski works in Silicon Valley. She attends a local Bible-based church and participates in various church related ministries.

She was first diagnosed with degenerative disc disease in 2007. She wrote this book after she found she was often consulted by people with neck and back problems and never had enough time to discuss all that she had learned and continues to learn about managing her back. By doing the things in this book, Tammi has been able to maintain an active lifestyle including playing volleyball, golfing, skiing, tap dancing and worship dancing.

Tammi has an MBA from the Anderson School of UCLA and a BSBA from Georgetown University in Accounting and International Management.

www.ingramcontent.com/pod-product-compliance
Lightning Source LLC
LaVergne TN
LVHW011243080426
835509LV00005B/614